P9-DHL-593

To Kati

Acknowledgments

One of those with an eye for emerging trends is Tom Lloyd, a like-minded author and thinker, who has been a source of inspiration for me ever since we collaborated on *Managing Know-How* (1987). Tom has improved the language and content of this book with his many contributions and suggestions.

I am also indebted to Brent Snow and Walter Johnston, who contributed American case material and insights. Both have supported my work with constructive dialogue and valuable, and much valued, advice.

I am grateful, too, to Charles Dorris, Libba Pinchot, Ron Cornman, and Tom Blanco, who reviewed the first drafts of the manuscript. Thank you! Thanks also to Alan Gilderson, who did the initial translation into English.

Last but not least I wish to thank my wife, Kati, doctor of ethnology. She has been an unfailing source of moral support and knowledgeable criticism from the earliest stages of my Ph.D. dissertation.

The New Organizational Wealth

MANAGING & MEASURING KNOWLEDGE-BASED ASSETS

Karl Erik Sveiby

Berrett-Koehler Publishers, Inc.
San Francisco

Copyright © 1997 by Karl Erik Sveiby
All rights reserved. No part of this publication may be reproduced, distributed, or transmitted in any form or by any means, including photocopying, recording, or other electronic or mechanical methods, without the prior written permission of the publisher, except in the case of brief quotations embodied in critical reviews and certain other noncommercial uses permitted by copyright law. For permission requests, write to the publisher, addressed "Attention: Permissions Coordinator" at the address below.

Berrett–Koehler Publishers, Inc.
450 Sansome Street, Suite 1200
San Francisco, CA 94111–3320
Tel: (415) 288–0260   Fax: (415) 362–2512

Ordering Information
Individual sales. Berrett–Koehler publications are available through most bookstores. They can also be ordered direct from Berrett–Koehler at the address above.

Quantity sales. Special discounts are available on quantity purchases by corporations, associations, and others. For details, contact the *Special Sales Department* at the Berrett–Koehler address above.

Orders for college textbook/course adoption use. Please contact Berrett–Koehler Publishers at the address above.

Orders by U.S. trade bookstores and wholesalers. Please contact Publishers Group West, 4065 Hollis Street, Box 8843, Emeryville, CA 94662. Tel: (510) 658–3453; 1–800–788–3123. Fax: (510) 658–1834

Printed in the United States of America
Printed on acid-free and recycled paper that is composed of 85% recovered fiber, including 15% postconsumer waste.

Library of Congress Cataloging–in–Publication Data
Sveiby, Karl Erik.
 The new organizational wealth: managing and measuring
knowledge–based assets / Karl Erik Sveiby.
   p. cm.
 Includes bibliographical references (p.) and index.
 ISBN 1-57675-014-0 (alk. paper)
  1. Intangible property–Management. 2. Intangible property–
Valuation. 3. Organization. 4. Information society. I. Title.
HD53.S893 1997
658–dc21   97–1964
           CIP

Printed in the United States of America
First Edition
99 98 97   10 9 8 7 6 5 4 3 2 1

Copyediting: Susan Beris
Indexing: Directions Unlimited
Proofreading: PeopleSpeak
Interior design and production: Joel Friedlander Publishing Services
Cover: Richard Adelson

The New Organizational Wealth

Contents

Preface

This book is a milestone in a continuing journey I began almost twenty years ago. In 1979, I left the secure, well-managed orderliness of a job at Unilever to hazard my luck and my career in what was, for me, the alien world of financial publishing. I joined a group of friends as a partner and manager to buy the fledgling Swedish business weekly, *Affärsvärlden*. There were 10 of us at the time. When we sold the company in 1994 we were 160 people, and the company, re-named E+T Frlag (Business and Technical Publishing), had seven titles and was one of Scandinavia's largest specialist publishing groups. Afterward, I went back to school to try to make some sense of my fifteen years as editor and manager by finishing my pending Ph.D.

In 1979, I had no idea of what I was letting myself in for. I thought that managing a small company with a few tangible assets would be a piece of cake; I was utterly wrong. Nothing had prepared me for the nonmanufacturing world—certainly neither the business school I had once attended nor the management literature I read so avidly, and least of all my management experience at Unilever. At the time I still believed that "real" companies had formal structures, that managers were in control and output was visible, and that the balance sheet gave a reasonably accurate account of the value of business.

At *Affärsvärlden*, we had no organization; we focused on the editorial content and outsourced everything else. We had no managers— I was the only one with managerial experience and I couldn't understand what was going on, let alone manage it. We had no visible production—we wrote in one city and the journal was printed in another. We had a formidable competitor in *Veckans Affärer*, owned by Sweden's largest and richest publishing group. We had no real assets and the balance sheet was a joke; there was no visible equity, and the brand name of the journal was valued in the accounts at a nominal one Swedish kronor. But we did have one thing: substantial *invisible knowledge-based* assets, including some of Sweden's best financial analysts, a well-known brand, and a large network of friends and well-wishers in the business community.

After I discovered that the conceptual tools that I had acquired in my earlier career were useless, I decided to start again with a blank sheet of paper. My curiosity about the nature of the organization I had become part of led me to seek out and interview leaders of similar companies who had been compelled, by their lack of tangible assets, to pay much closer attention to their intangible, knowledge-based assets. I began to realize that what distinguished such people most clearly from their counterparts in manufacturing firms was their different perception of their businesses. They took little notice of the financials and were more concerned about their people, their networks, and their image. Furthermore, it was clear that the number of leaders who saw their firms in this way was growing rapidly.

While at the magazine, I changed jobs several times—from accountant to financial journalist to stock market editor to database manager to management journalist to publisher to executive chairman—remaining one of the managing partners throughout. I became fascinated by the issue of managing intangible assets. In 1986, I wrote my first book on the subject, in Swedish: *Kunskapsföretaget (The Know-How Company)*. I believe that I have since acquired a deeper understanding of the knowledge company, but my original observation remains valid: managers in some of the fastest-growing and most profitable businesses focus on knowledge, see their businesses from a knowledge perspective, and act as if their intangible assets are real assets. By freeing themselves from the mental straitjackets of the industrial age, some of these pioneer managers have found, seemingly by accident sometimes, a wellspring of limitless resources arising from the infinite human ability to create knowledge and from the convenient fact that, unlike conventional assets, knowledge grows when it is shared.

Yet most of these pioneers lack explicit tools; they manage intuitively, by gut feeling. I have seen it as my task over the past fifteen years to make explicit some of their tacit knowledge in order to supply them, as well as less experienced knowledge managers and other interested parties, with a toolbox of knowledge management skills to make their lives a little easier. These pioneers are traveling in uncharted territory, and most of them lack even a basic theory of knowledge—an epistemology, as philosophers call it. It's as if managers and management authors shy away from a task that has engaged the interest of philosophers since the dawn of human thought. I believe the managers of knowledge companies must suppress their natural distaste for philosophizing and confront the need for a theory of knowledge.

I have therefore devoted Chapters 3 and 4 in Part I of this book to an exploration of the twin concepts of *knowledge* and *information*.

We must look anew at these two concepts and the relationships between them. On the basis of my experience in the media industry, I argue that the widespread assumption in our modern age of information technology that information is meaningful and valuable is a completely and dangerously incorrect assumption.

While I urge managers to adopt a knowledge perspective and to see their firms' invisible balance sheets of intangible assets, I also emphasize that knowledge organizations do not constitute a class of firm. Rather, the term is a label signifying a family of organizations that share common features. Chapters 3 and 4 discuss this issue in rather theoretical terms. Busy readers may be tempted to skip them. But I advise readers to persevere because these epistemological concepts and tools will shed new light on most managerial areas.

Part II moves on to more practical matters with a discussion of the management of intangible assets. I only have space to cover a few strategic points of this vast topic in this book.

Part III offers a toolbox for measuring intangible assets based on the conceptual framework outlined in earlier chapters. It describes how WM-data, one of Europe's most successful software and consulting firms, has used the concepts and measurements outlined in this book to monitor its operations for many years. It includes brief descriptions of other Scandinavian firms that have begun to tackle the problems of measuring and presenting intangible assets.

I have been researching ways to measure intangible assets for a decade now. My work in Sweden has inspired a number of Scandinavian companies to monitor their intangible assets according to the principles I outline. They have found that the problem is not how to design the indicators—there are plenty of them already—but how to interpret them. It takes several years to leave old perspectives behind and the transition period can be frustrating. Because we see what we measure, firms using measurement systems based on obsolete perspectives are managing by way of a rearview mirror. They preserve the past instead of managing for the future.

Thus this book begins in Chapters 1 and 2 by introducing the concept of intangible assets and describing the conceptual framework of the knowledge organization of which they are a part. For until you understand your company, you do not know how to manage it or what to measure, and you have no way of knowing where it is or could be going.

To those interested in continuing a dialogue with me after they conclude the book, I extend an invitation to visit my Web site at http://www.eis.net.au/~karlerik/index.html. It contains much more on this subject than I have been able to squeeze between the covers of this book. Comments may also be e-mailed to karlerik@eis.net.au.

The Era of the Knowledge Organization

The Era of the Knowledge Organization

Chapter 1 introduces the concept of intangible assets and their three components:

- Employee competence
- Internal structure
- External structure

However, before managing or measuring a company's intangible assets, one must be able to "see" an organization as a knowledge organization, that is, to see the business from the standpoint of knowledge, see it as consisting of nothing but knowledge in the broadest sense, and see that it is the manager's job to develop and manage this knowledge. A special perspective is needed to filter out the tangible and reveal what, by definition, is the essence of a knowledge organization.

To help readers achieve a knowledge perspective, Chapters 2 through 4 discuss the characteristics of doing business in the current knowledge era, the concept of knowledge, and the ways in which knowledge is transferred from person to person.

The New Wealth:
Intangible Assets

Shares in Microsoft, the world's largest computer software firm, changed hands at an average price of $70 during 1995 at a time when their so-called book value or equity was just $7. In other words, for every $1 of recorded value the market saw $9 in additional value for which there was no corresponding record in Microsoft's balance sheet.

What is it about Microsoft that makes it worth ten times the value of its recorded assets? What is the nature of that additional value that is perceived by the market but not recorded by the company? Or, to generalize the question, why do some companies have higher market-to-book ratios than others?

Stock analysts, the most influential arbiters of corporate value, will say that the reason for Microsoft's high market-to-book ratio is the firm's extraordinary profitability—it achieved a return on equity of almost 30 percent in 1995—and its phenomenal growth record. But this does not answer the question, it just rephrases it. Why is Microsoft so profitable and why has it grown so fast? What is the mysterious, hugely productive asset that Microsoft clearly has and that Ford Motor Company and Bethlehem Steel, whose shares trade close to their book values, lack?

Microsoft's annual report, the definitive and official statement of the company's affairs, provides no explanation. The 1995 report, for example, is full of fine pictures and eloquent words about brilliant products and bright futures, but there is not even a hint about the nature of the mysterious asset. The company's financial statements are no more illuminating. They're packed with figures, but none offer investors any explanation of why Microsoft's shares trade at $63 above their tangible asset value. Indeed, even though the market obviously perceives Microsoft as an entirely different kind of company, its financial statements do not differ in any substantial way from those of Ford Motor Company or Bethlehem Steel.

The problem with stock market mysteries of this kind is that investors are obliged to develop their own explanations for them. They can see the previous year's cash flow because it is recorded in the financials, but when it comes to assessing changes in the value of the intangible assets that will help to generate future cash flows, they are on their own.

As a consequence of this ill-informed investor guessing, the market values of companies rich in intangible assets tend to fluctuate a lot, in line with general economic cycles and the mood among investors. Microsoft and other firms with high market-to-book ratios are like icebergs, bobbing up and down as investors change their views about what might be going on under the surface.

Sun Microsystems is a case in point. This company is best known for designing and manufacturing workstations, network computer systems, and microprocessors. It is recognized as one of the larger hardware producers in Silicon Valley—successful, but not unique. The explanation for the huge difference between Sun's net book value and stock market value in 1995 and 1996 shown in Figure 1 cannot be found among Sun's hardware products.

The real reason for this dichotomy is that Sun is also a big player in software development for networks and network-related computer services and when the implication of Java—the hot new software for Internet applications that Sun developed—dawned upon investors, they pushed up the company's stock valuation by $4.4 billion in eighteen months. Nothing happened in the profit pattern and little happened in tangible terms to justify that enormous change. Nevertheless, Sun in 1996 is regarded as an entirely different company than Sun in 1994.

This revaluation reflects that Sun is no longer regarded as a manufacturer of workstations. The stock market believes that Java is Sun's ticket to the casino of technology, where it may play the game of increasing returns, as economist Brian Arthur (1996) puts it. (See Chapter 2 for more on this.) The revaluation also reflects the presence of invisible or intangible assets.

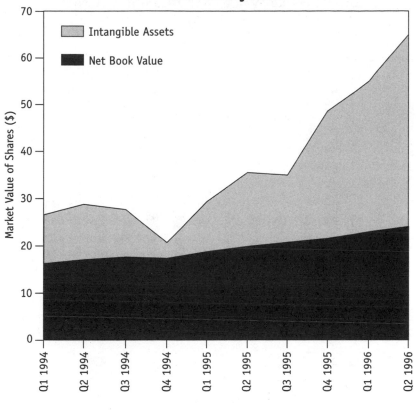

Sun Microsystems

Market Value of Shares ($)

- Intangible Assets
- Net Book Value

Q1 1994, Q2 1994, Q3 1994, Q4 1994, Q1 1995, Q2 1995, Q3 1995, Q4 1995, Q1 1996, Q2 1996

Figure 1. The difference between Sun Microsystems' stock market value and net book value reflects the importance of its intangible assets.

▪ᵗ Invisible Assets: A Broad-Based Phenomenon

As shown in Figures 2 and 3, high proportions of intangible assets to market value are by no means confined to companies participating in information technology or the so-called high–tech industries with companies like Microsoft, Intel, or Genentech. In fact, in 1995 many electronics companies had a fairly low proportion of intangible assets to market value (Oxford Instruments, Hewlett–Packard) compared with those of media companies (Springer, Reuters), waste management firms (Rentokil), and many branded consumer products companies (Coca–Cola, Unilever, Hugo Boss, Arnotts), which all had high proportions.

Pharmaceutical companies (for example, Astra, Glaxo) generally had higher proportions than service companies (for example, Wal-

Global Market Values and Intangible Assets
April 1995

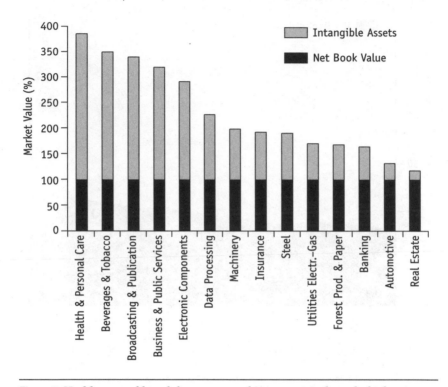

Figure 2. Health care and branded consumer products companies have the highest intangible assets. In contrast, in real estate, most of the assets are tangible and therefore measured. Source: Morgan & Stanley Capital International World Index.

Mart, McDonald's), whereas companies whose mission is to manage tangible assets like banks and financial services (Citicorp, American Express) or real estate (Energy Resources) were typically valued at or near their visible equity. Other industries with low market appreciation of their intangible assets were the traditional manufacturing industries, including the automotive industry (Ford Motor Company, Volvo, Daimler–Benz), and chemical firms (BASF).

That the difference between market value and book value has less to do with tangible than intangible assets is underlined by a comparison between Bethlehem Steel and Nucor, the company that revolutionized the steel industry with its minimill approach. Whereas Bethlehem Steel is in most respects a traditional steel manufacturer, Nucor's prime assets are its new minimill technology and a

Market Values and Intangible Assets
April 1995

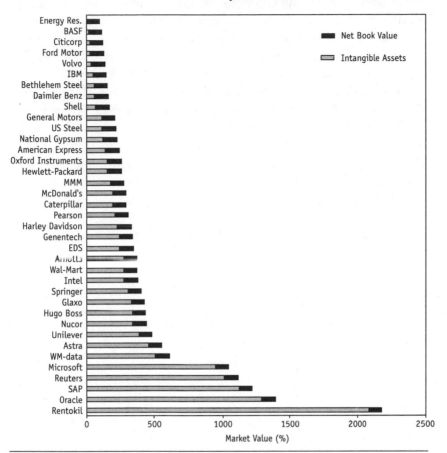

Figure 3. High-tech companies are not the only ones to have a high proportion of intangible assets. The bar for each company consists of tangible assets (converted to 100 percent for comparative purposes) and intangible assets (market value less tangible assets).

management approach that releases the competence of its employees. Nucor and Bethlehem had roughly the same tangible assets—net book values of $1.3 billion and $1.2 billion, respectively, in November 1995. But Nucor's superior intangible assets delivered a 17 percent net return on equity in 1994 compared with Bethelem Steel's 3 percent. Consequently, the stock market priced Nucor at a total valuation of $4.6 billion and Bethlehem Steel at a mere $1.7 billion.

Companies do not trade their intangible assets, so the value of intangible assets cannot be deduced like the value of tangible assets from routine market transactions. The value only emerges in this indirect way on the stock market or when a company changes hands. For example, when one company acquires another and pays a premium over its book value, accounting theory terms that premium *goodwill.* (Accounting theory and measurement are discussed in more detail in Part III.) The amount of goodwill is entered as a lump sum in the books and depreciated over up to forty years.

The stock market provides a daily valuation of the assets of listed companies and approximates the goodwill that would be measured in if the whole company were to be acquired. Stock market values fluctuate because of general economic trends, of course, and one single snapshot of a market does not tell the full truth. Still, the company valuations cited in this chapter illustrate my arguments.

The stock market price of a company is the market's valuation of the shares in the equity. Each share certificate represents a share in the company's equity or book value. When the market price is higher than the book value, conventional stock market theory regards the premium as the market's assessment of future earning potential, a potential that is converted into goodwill if the company is acquired. So there must be something among the company's assets that will yield higher than bank interest in the future. These assets are *invisible* because they are not accounted for. They are *intangible* because they are neither brick nor mortar nor money.

Nevertheless, these invisible, intangible assets need not be a mystery. They all derive from an organization's personnel. Furthermore, these assets can be classified into three types that together form a balance sheet of intangible assets.

⬤ The Three Types of Intangible Assets

People are the only true agents in business. All assets and structures—whether tangible or intangible—are the result of human actions. All depend ultimately on people for their continued existence.

People are constantly extending themselves into their world through tangible means, as when they cultivate gardens or buy houses and cars, and through intangible means, as when they create ideas and develop relationships with corporations and other people.

Marshall "The Medium Is the Message" McLuhan (1967) called these intangible extensions *media*. It was McLuhan who in this way made me understand that individuals in organizations create what I call *external* and *internal structures* to express themselves.[1]

In brief, if the managers of a car company or a soap company direct the efforts of their people inward, they will create intangible internal structures, like better processes or new product designs. If they direct attention outward, in addition to producing tangible things like cars or soap, they will create intangible external structures like customer relationships.

In fact, production often has as much or more to do with creating knowledge structures as with creating material production. Product distribution often has as much or more to do with creating knowledge jointly with customers as with transporting the physical product. Some assets—like brand names, customer relationships, and the competence of employees—are best seen as knowledge structures, that is, intangible assets.

The duty of a manager is to develop the assets of the organization. But difficulties arise when an organization's most valuable assets are not material objects like machinery, real estate, and factories, which are owned by the company and appear in its balance sheet, but are intangible and therefore invisible.

Yet the economic value of a customer or supplier relationship is not really more invisible than the market value of a factory. So why is such a relationship treated as invisible? Because it lacks a generally accepted definition and a measurement standard. These drawbacks do not mean that it is impossible or unnecessary to measure a relationship, only that comparisons between companies and over time are difficult to make. One goal of this book is to help managers overcome this difficulty by allowing them to see and to classify their intangible assets.

Again, people in an organization direct their efforts in two directions primarily: outward working with customers or inward maintaining and building the organization. When they work with customers they create customer relationships and an image in the marketplace that is partly "owned" by the corporation. I call this an external structure. When their efforts are directed inward they create an internal structure, which in management literature is called the organization. I regard both as structures of knowledge.

The structures are partly independent of individuals; some structure remains even if a large number of employees leave. Indeed, even if the most valuable individuals leave a company that depends heavily on individuals (a consulting firm, for example), at least parts of the internal and external structures will probably remain intact, such as the organization's name, software, manuals, registers, and so on, which can serve as a platform for a new start.

In sum, the invisible assets on an organization's balance sheet can be classified as a family of three: *employee competence, internal structure, and external structure.*[2, 3]

EMPLOYEE COMPETENCE

Employee competence involves the capacity to act in a wide variety of situations to create both tangible and intangible assets. Some may not agree that employee competence is an intangible asset. It is true that individual competence cannot be owned by anyone or anything except the person who possesses it; when all is said and done employees are voluntary members of an organization.

Nevertheless, employee competence should be included in the balance sheet of intangible assets because it is impossible to conceive of an organization without people. Furthermore, people tend to be loyal if they are treated fairly and feel a sense of shared responsibility. That is why companies are generally willing to give compensation to those who retire or are laid off. This kind of compensation varies from country to country but often takes the form of severance pay, umbrella agreements (including "golden parachutes"), and pensions. Although such commitments are not recorded as liabilities on the balance sheet, they can be seen as pledges or commitments, like lease or rental contracts, and thus a form of invisible financing of employee competence.

In a knowledge organization, there is little machinery other than the employees. Because only people can act, employees become both the minders of the machines and the machines themselves.

INTERNAL STRUCTURE

The internal structure includes patents, concepts, models, and computer and administrative systems. These are created by the employees and are generally owned by the organization. Sometimes they can be acquired elsewhere. Decisions to develop or invest in such assets can be made with some degree of confidence because the work is done in-house or brought in from outside.

In addition, the organizational culture or spirit is also an internal structure.

The internal structure and the people together constitute what is generally called the organization. People create the organization by interacting with each other and thus enacting the environment (Weick 1977). (This concept is discussed further in Chapter 2.)

EXTERNAL STRUCTURE

The external structure includes relationships with customers and suppliers. It also encompasses brand names, trademarks, and the company's reputation or image. Some of these can be considered legal property, but investments in external structure cannot be made with the same degree of confidence as investments in internal structure. The value of these assets is primarily determined by how well the company solves its customers' problems, so there is always an element of uncertainty here. Reputations and relationships can change over time.

◗ The Balance Sheet of Intangible Assets

Figure 4 shows a balance sheet indicating the three families of intangible assets along with the material or visible assets that make up the familiar balance sheet seen in annual reports. It itemizes material assets and shows how they are financed.

The heretofore invisible balance sheet consists of employee competence and internal and external structures. These intangible assets have a substantial implication for financing a knowledge organiza-

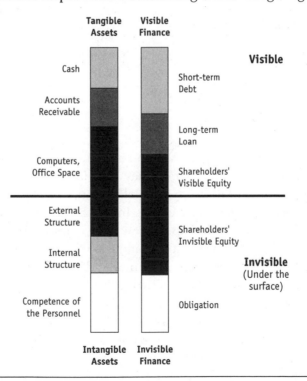

Figure 4. The balance sheet of a knowledge organization.

tion. Visible financing is usually very simple: it consists of equity (shareholders' capital), short-term loans, and a few long-term loans, which are often difficult to arrange because a lack of tangible collateral makes banks uneasy. Because of the reluctance of banks to lend for investment in intangible assets, the development of knowledge organizations is mostly self-financed; in other words, the invisible assets are financed mostly with invisible equity (the difference between book value and market value) and with contingent obligations to employees (severance pay, golden parachutes, and so on).

⸬ Seeing Intangible Assets

Thus, although intangible assets may seem invisible, they can actually be discerned quite easily. A core argument of this book is that it is possible to classify intangible assets within these three families: *external structure, internal structure,* and *competence of the employees.* Exhibit 1 summarizes these in table form.

	Intangible Assets (Stock price premium)		
Visible Equity (book value) Tangible assets minus visible debt.	**External structure** (brands, customer and supplier relations)	**Internal structure** (the organization: management, legal structure, manual systems, attitudes, R&D, software)	**Individual competence** (education, experience)

Exhibit 1. The total market value of a company can be seen to consist of its visible equity and three kinds of intangible assets.

If consumer goods companies—Coca-Cola, for example—are classified in this way, it is reasonable to assume that the intangible assets lie mainly in the brand names they own (an external structure), the established organization (an internal structure), and perhaps the original recipes (an internal structure). Intangible assets like well-known brand names or technical know-how have commercial value because they are owned by the company and thus survive individuals.

McDonald's most valuable intangible assets are probably its brand name and franchise network (both external structures). The market value of a car manufacturer like Ford Motor Company probably consists largely of its tangible assets and its long-established managerial experience in organizing complex production (an internal structure). A construction company's main asset, if it does not own real estate, is its ability to carry out complex projects (an internal structure).

The intangible assets of pharmaceutical companies like Merck and Pharmacia–Upjohn lie in their R&D portfolios (an internal structure) and brand names (an external structure), while their production is not that complex. The value of a consulting firm like EDI or Arthur Andersen (if it were listed on the stock exchange) lies mainly in the competence of its staff and its relationships with its customers. For these firms, tangible assets and visible equity would count for little of the value.

Microsoft's huge share–price premium over book value, at some $45 billion in 1995, is primarily attributed to its customer base in the form of thirty–five million people who use its Windows operating system. These customers can be seen as a captive audience because it is hard to switch from one operating system to another. They are therefore likely to buy Microsoft's software in the future.

Indeed, intangible assets are so valuable that if managers do not know how to manage them, they will lead the company into disaster. Consider, for example, the rise and fall of Saatchi & Saatchi, which, for a few months in 1988, was the largest advertising agency in the world. Yet it lost its way when its managers focused on financial capital—a tangible asset—instead of on its intangible assets.

⸫ Saatchi & Saatchi: Intangible Assets Lost

In December 1994 Maurice Saatchi left his office on Charlotte Street, London, for the last time. He had been forced to resign as chairman of Saatchi & Saatchi—the advertising group that he and his elder brother Charles had founded in 1970—by a group of disenchanted investors. Maurice was livid with fury and made no secret about it. "For the first time in twenty–five years," he wrote in a resignation letter that he later issued to the press, "I found myself in an agency where the term *advertising man* was being used as an insult."

Maurice Saatchi's resignation was the culmination of a series of problems the firm had experienced. Saatchi & Saatchi had its initial public offering (IPO) on the London stock exchange in 1976. It was the first advertising business to overcome the city's perception of the advertising industry as "arty," as all glitter, no substance. Thanks almost entirely to the eloquence of the Saatchi brothers and the persuasive powers of their original finance director, Martin Sorrell (whose WPP Group would later overtake Saatchi & Saatchi as the world's largest advertising agency), investors both in London and on Wall Street learned to see advertising as an industry with reliable profitability and good growth potential that could be leveraged further by acquisitions.

The Saatchi brothers also worked their magic within the firm by containing the powerful centrifugal forces endemic in the profession. While delivering profits, growth, and dividends to their new outside shareholders, they managed to preserve a creative spirit, which is the essence of good advertising.

Their story of uninterrupted success lasted ten years—from 1976 to 1986—during which period they acquired other agencies at a rate of three per year. The peak came in April 1986 when, through a secondary issue of stock, investors paid 400 million pounds for a 47 percent share of the company. A month later, the money was used to buy the New York agency Ted Bates. It was with this deal that the brothers achieved their goal of becoming the world's largest advertising group, with billings of $7.5 billion.

Until then, surprisingly few key people—notably the founders and creative leaders of acquired agencies—had left. Such loyalty was partly the result of the pioneering culture the brothers had created and partly of a system of deferred payments, or "earn–outs," devised by Sorrell. Instead of immediately receiving all of an agreed–upon sum for selling their agencies, owners were paid a portion in cash and promised further payments later on, linked to the subsequent performance of the acquired business. It was a clever system because it not only reduced the initial cost of an acquisition but also gave the former owners every incentive to stay on and maximize the value of the subsequent payments. The trouble with the earn–out system was that it accumulated a large, contingent liability on Saatchi & Saatchi's balance sheet that could—and, as chance would have it, did—become payable during a period when cash was tight and the stock market too weak for an additional issue of equity.

The Ted Bates deal was a turning point because of its size. A few key accounts were immediately lost because of conflicts of interest between Saatchi & Saatchi and Ted Bates clients. Because these were not wholly offset by new business, the 1986 results recorded the group's first-ever profit decline.

By then a leakage of creative talent had also begun. Many Ted Bates professionals were infuriated by the merger and some said so publicly. The staff of the Ted Bates agency in France circulated a picture of a pregnant man (from a famous Saatchi & Saatchi antismoking campaign) that carried the caption *"Nous sommes baisés"* ("We've been screwed"). The magic that for so long had maintained the creative integrity of the Saatchi & Saatchi group had begun to fade.

But still in the grip of their hubris, the brothers continued to expand their empire. In early 1987, they announced a new, even bolder strategy of becoming a global one-stop shop of business services including marketing, financial services, and management consulting in addition to advertising. New acquisitions would follow in these areas.

In the summer of 1987, Tom Lloyd and I predicted the demise of the Saatchi empire in our book, *Managing Know-How*, on the grounds that the firm's strategy violated the business logic of knowledge organizations.

The brothers were not deterred by the warning, however; they even quoted from our book in a subsequent annual statement. Later that year, they made it known that they were interested in buying Midland Bank, one of the United Kingdom's "big four" retail banks. This was too much for a financial community already concerned by the fallout from the Ted Bates deal. The company's stock market image, so vital to its acquisition strategy, went into a decline from which it has yet to recover.

But at the end of 1988, the group's market capitalization was still 636 million pounds, compared with net assets of 108 million pounds. So for every pound of tangible assets investors were still adding another five to reflect intangible assets. The intangible assets continued to leak away, however. It was not long before the hemorrhage of talent began to affect Saatchi & Saatchi's reputation within the profession as a top creative performer. It became harder to attract and keep good people and good clients. Frustration among the executives was further fueled by lackluster performance of the shares, as shown in Figure 5.

By 1989 the Saatchi group was in financial crisis. The banks organized a major financial restructuring and brought in a professional manager to oversee daily operations. He cut costs and sold what were considered to be noncore businesses, but losses still mounted. By 1993, they were running at 20 million pounds a year, and high-profile clients, including Chrysler and Helene Curtis, continued to defect. A new operations manager cut executive pay, persuaded Charles Saatchi to withdraw, moved the head office to lower-rent premises, and launched a compulsory layoff program that cost 10 million pounds in severance pay.

Saatchi & Saatchi Share Price

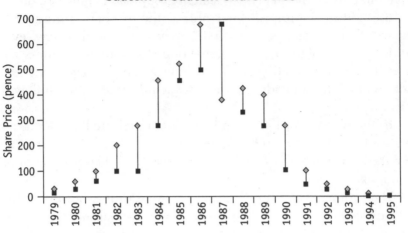

Figure 5. Saatchi & Saatchi share price development illustrates the danger of disregarding the value of intangible assets. Source: Datastream.

If not the beginning of the end for Saatchi & Saatchi—which has since been renamed Cordiant—Maurice Saatchi's departure at the end of 1994 was another body blow. Determined to make fools of his persecutors, he started a new agency with his brother and began to compete with them. In the aftermath of what was quickly billed "the nightmare on Charlotte Street," Cordiant lost 40 million pounds of business (6 percent of total billings), much of which, including the British Airways, Dixons, and Mars accounts, went to the brothers' new agency, M&C Saatchi.

Cordiant's shareholders, some of whom had joined with Chicago fund manager David Herro to oust Maurice, could only watch in dismay as the value of their company plunged to barely 2 percent of its peak market capitalization attained in 1988.

LESSONS TO BE LEARNED

The eighteen years of extraordinary, almost uninterrupted growth at Saatchi & Saatchi suggest that the advertising business is much like any other. The firm's strategy was based on two ideas: first, customers can buy all kinds of professional advice from one source and, second, economies of scale exist in creative problem solving just as they do in manufacturing.

But the dramatic fall of the house of Saatchi & Saatchi suggests otherwise. It suggests that creative problem solving is not at all like other businesses and can offer very little in the way of economies of scale. But if that much is now clear, there remains the question of how the two brothers managed to defy the laws of creative gravity for so long.

The answer lies in their "bank account" of intangible assets. When the firm went public, Saatchi & Saatchi employed a number of very skilled advertising professionals, had a collection of high-profile customers, and had an image of being creative. Supported by their profit track record, the Saatchi brothers managed to persuade a reluctant London business community that advertising was just like any other industry, driven by the same business logic as, say, manufacturing. They converted parts of their intangible assets into cash in their initial public offering. This gave them a high share rating, which they used brilliantly in an aggressive acquisition strategy.

Another part of the answer lies in the commonsense mindset of the brothers. That is, they took the view that the company *had* to be profitable, that profit growth was the only measure of its success, and that the reward for success was a lower cost for the financial capital that all companies need.

Saatchi & Saatchi did need financial capital, but not for the advertising business. It needed it for acquisitions. In fact, the Saatchi brothers left the advertising business the moment they began to use the agency network as a vehicle for buying nonadvertising businesses.

Yes, profit growth in their original advertising business was a sign of success, reflected in what I call *organic growth* in the years before 1976. This healthy growth was generated by satisfied customers demanding more of their competence. In contrast, after the IPO, most of the growth came from acquisitions. But the London business community failed to recognize the difference between organic growth and acquired growth. For a long time, Saatchi &Saatchi seemed to ride the crest of a volume wave that produced more profits, boosted the share price, created more opportunities for acquisition, and so on.

The Saatchi case reveals the dangers of ignoring or failing to understand the value and nature of intangible assets. The firm's intangible assets were like a bank account that it slowly depleted after it went public. The London business community and Wall Street did not (and still do not) comprehend how the management of intangible assets such as knowledge, competence, and image (or reputation) create tangible profits. That the Saatchi brothers did understand it at one time is demonstrated by the success of the business before and immediately after the IPO. But their subsequent acquisition strategy was based on their belief that advertising is like any other industry, driven by the same logic as manufacturing. Once they went public, they adopted a tycoon mindset, forgetting all they had learned and becoming unconscious of (or choosing to ignore) the damage the new strategy was inflicting on their three key intangible assets.

Thus, they lost *competence* when people left and became their competitors; they lost *external structure* when their creative reputation slipped and prestigious customers defected; and they lost *internal structure* when their organization began to resemble a pyramid turned upside down—retaining key people was based on promises for future profits and when those promises came due but could not be met, the structure fell apart.

Could Saatchi & Saatchi have succeeded? Yes. As I argue in this book, if the brothers had adopted a knowledge-focused strategy, they would have realized that their intangible assets—contrary to the belief of their financial advisors—were more important than their tangible assets, and they might have acted differently. They would then have been supported by a wellspring of unlimited resources.

Summary

- The difference between the market value of a publicly held company and its official net book value is the value of its intangible assets. In most companies, the value of intangible assets exceeds the value of tangible assets.
- The invisible part of the balance sheet consists of three families of intangible assets: *employee competence*, or the capacity of employees to act in a wide variety of situations; *internal structure*, including patents, concepts, models, and computer and administrative systems, that is, the organization; and *external structures*, customer and supplier relationships and the organization's image.

Advice to Managers

- A manager's duty is to develop the assets of an organization, the intangible assets as well as the tangible ones.
- In order to "see" the knowledge organization, managers should try to regard their organizations as if they consisted of knowledge structures rather than of capital.

Tapping into the Limitless Resources of the Knowledge Era

Before going on to discuss how to manage and measure intangible assets, we must come to grips with what it actually means to do business in the knowledge era. This chapter discusses the characteristics of knowledge organizations, the products of knowledge organizations, and the management of knowledge organizations.[1]

▪ The Knowledge Organization

Both Microsoft and Saatchi & Saatchi are examples of a new breed of company that I call *knowledge organizations* or *knowledge companies*. Although their businesses seem worlds apart, they share some important characteristics.

Most employees of knowledge companies are highly qualified and highly educated professionals—that is, they are *knowledge workers*. Their work consists largely of converting information to knowledge, using their own competencies for the most part, sometimes with the assistance of suppliers of information or specialized knowledge. These companies have few tangible assets. Their intangible assets are much more valuable than their tangible assets.

Furthermore, knowledge organizations are not islands. They would not exist if not for local clusters of customers and suppliers that support and enhance their knowledge bases. Stanford University economist Brian Arthur calls such networks *miniecologies;* in this book, these relationships fall under the rubric of external structures. External structures are based not so much on financial flows as on knowledge flows created by intangible assets.

Finally, if we assume that the professional services or business services sector is a close equivalent of knowledge organizations, then the growth of knowledge organizations has been rapid and sustained. In fact, knowledge organizations are growing so fast that, as shown in Figure 6, their numbers are overtaking those of the manufacturing sector.

Employment in USA
Share of Total Employment

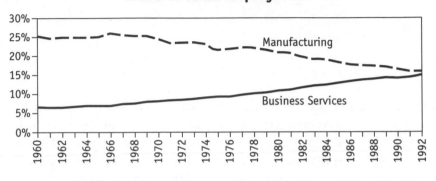

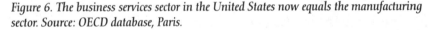

Figure 6. The business services sector in the United States now equals the manufacturing sector. Source: OECD database, Paris.

Thus, the business services sector is a heterogeneous, rapidly growing group of small enterprises[2] selling knowledge, information, and other services, primarily to other businesses. Published statistics bunch firms such as advertising agencies, law and accounting firms, and engineering and management consultants together with real estate brokers, computer consultants, and—in some countries—software producers.

The year 1995 may well be remembered in the United States as the year when companies *serving* industry for the first time outnumbered those *working in* industry. According to Organization for Economic Cooperation and Development (OECD) statistics, the U.S. business services sector has grown steadily over the years, now employing some eighteen million people—as many as the entire manufacturing sector. Fifty percent of the fastest-growing companies in the United States between 1989 and 1993 could be labeled knowledge companies. Less than a fifth were manufacturers and the rest were in trade or other types of service. Because official industrial statistics are still based on outdated industry models that assume that manufacturing plays the dominant role, they do not track these trends well. Nevertheless, there is enough evidence of rapid and sustained growth in business and professional services to conclude with some confidence that knowledge companies make up the world's most rapidly growing business sector. Indeed, although statistics in this area are somewhat unreliable and slow in coming, it looks as if the same pattern prevails in all OECD economies, with the United States leading the pack. (See Figure 7.)

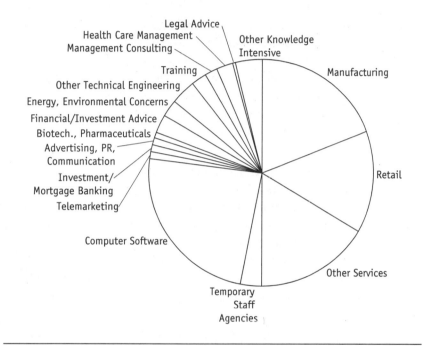

Figure 7. Fifty percent of the fastest-growing companies in the United States can be described as knowledge companies. Source: INC 500, 1995.

The growth appears robust because it is sustained even in hard times. In the small economy of Sweden, the numbers of people employed in the professional services sector doubled to 220,000 between 1980 and 1992, and the growth did not falter even when the economy hit bottom in 1991–92. Whereas manufacturing employment fell by 13 percent between the boom year of 1989 and the crisis year of 1992, employment in professional services rose by precisely the same percentage during that period, according to the Swedish Council of Service Industries.

◄ The Products of the Knowledge Organization

In the mid-1980s, Brian Arthur observed three characteristics of the products emerging from Silicon Valley's booming software industry:

1. Like pharmaceutical and other high-tech products, the software produced had very high developmental costs but very low production costs.

2. Customers valued compatibility in these software products. Thus, once market share was won, it became easier to sell upgrades or add-ons.

3. Once users mastered one software package, they were reluctant to change to another. Learning a software package takes time; files created in one format are not easily transferred to another. Thus, Microsoft and other software developers combatted this phenomenon by offering competitive upgrades; owners of competing software could buy the Microsoft version at a large discount. It is this strategy that has enabled Microsoft to dominate the personal computer software market for so long.

NO LAW OF DIMINISHING RETURNS

Microsoft's success appears to violate a time-honored economic principle—the law of diminishing returns. According to this principle, as long as output increases there will come a time when costs per unit will begin to rise too. This principle is valid in a world of limited physical resources, that is, for those industries involved in bulk processes, for example. Such industries are now dominated by large companies, and if these companies try to expand they run into some kind of limitation, be it in numbers of consumers who prefer their brand, access to raw materials, or something else. Returns start falling because the expansion costs outweigh the extra margin gained.

But if the cost of developing software is the same whether one copy of the product is sold or one million copies are sold, the market leaders will always make more money than the runners-up. Unlike land, oil, or iron, information and knowledge are not intrinsically scarce. They can be conjured up by human minds from nothing. The cost of the physical input—food—needed to maintain the creative process is negligible. Also unlike oil and iron, knowledge and information grow when shared; an idea or skill shared with someone else is not lost but doubled. An economy based on knowledge and information has unlimited resources.

KNOWLEDGE GROWS FROM SHARING

Also unlike goods and services, knowledge does not disappear when it is sold. If you sell me a vacuum cleaner, I take the machine away from you and you get my money in return. If you sell me a train ticket or rent me a hotel room, the seat on the train and the bed in the room are subject to wear and tear because of my use of them. Thus, capital depreciates with use, but knowledge appreciates. Your stock of knowledge is not diminished if you share it with me. If I hire you to help my people develop their abilities, you will not only keep your knowledge after you have "sold" it but will probably have learned something new from my people in the process.

COMMUNICATION AND PERSONAL CHEMISTRY

But knowledge is not a simple business. For example, if you analyze the market for cars in China and produce a report for me on the subject, what I am buying from you is not really the neatly bound, well-illustrated report, but rather the ability to make better decisions in order to gain improved results for my business. If no such improvement occurs and I feel that the inadequacy of your work is partly to blame for the disappointment, I will feel cheated. Success in the delicate business of transferring human competence thus depends to a very large extent on how well knowledge vendors communicate with their customers. Since the effectiveness of human communication depends as much on the personal chemistry between communicators as on the clarity or quality of the reports that pass between them, how well particular people suit particular customers—and vice versa—is just as important if not more important than the quality and quantity of the knowledge to be imparted.

Brian Arthur is one of few economists to have studied the economy of knowledge, and he has incorporated some of the basic principles of knowledge and information into an economic theory. We're still some way from a coherent model of a knowledge economy. One of the major flaws is that Arthur, like many other economists, confuses information with knowledge. Nevertheless, I shall use Arthur's theory to illuminate the business of managing intangible assets.

The increasing returns game in the software market is a high-risk, high-return, winner-takes-all game; in fact, it is almost digital, like the information embedded in the software. In contrast, as we will see, the market for knowledge is very different.

THE DIFFERENCE BETWEEN INFORMATION AND KNOWLEDGE

Although software development and advertising firms share several characteristics, there is an important difference between them. Software companies bundle the knowledge of their employees into standardized packages of information, and as already discussed, once they have produced the prototype, further copies cost next to nothing. In contrast, the output of advertising firms is problem solving. This requires intimate dialogue—what Bill Gates calls high bandwidth communication—between expert and customer. No customer wants the same ad twice, so the wonderful world of zero-cost production is out of reach. Because there are no standard problems, consultants must treat their customers as individuals. Because consultants cannot standardize their customers, they must either seek customers their people can serve or seek people who can serve their customers.

This distinction between organizations that sell knowledge as a package and those that sell knowledge as a process is vitally important. Even if both rely heavily on intangible assets for their success, the art of achieving increasing returns is different. One is driven by *information*, the other is driven by *knowledge*.

Some of the present confusion concerning how to do business in the knowledge era would probably be eliminated if we had a better understanding of the ways in which information and knowledge are both similar and different. The widespread but largely unconscious assumption that information is equal to knowledge and that the relationship between a computer and information is equivalent to the relationship between a human brain and human knowledge can lead to dangerous and costly mistakes. For example, it had cost Japan's computer industry a bundle by the time it decided to abandon its attempt to build a fifth-generation computer, or artificial brain. The mistaken idea that knowledge exists in some way and, like information in databases, can be "reengineered" as easily as signals transmitted from computer to computer has similarly cost money and caused pain to many.

▪▪ Managing the Knowledge Organization

Many claim that America is evolving into a new kind of society in which most work is knowledge work. The evidence, such as it is, suggests that other OECD countries are following suit.

The environment that managers will have to work in in the future has been eloquently described by many authors. They outline a new and dangerous society, age, or era. They label it "the third wave" (Toffler 1980), "the information society" (Masuda 1980), "the knowledge society" (Masuda 1980, Naisbitt 1982), and "the postcapitalist era" (Drucker 1993). It will be the virtual (Rheingold 1993) knowledge era (Savage 1995) characterized by the smart machine (Zuboff 1988) and "unreason" (Handy 1990).

This new world is already presenting challenges for managers. Classical management theory assumes that leaders make decisions and subordinates carry them out, that talk is one thing and action another, and that leaders are always better informed than the staff— or can easily become so—because they control the flow of information. This theory assumes, in short, that the bosses are in charge.

But suppose classical theory is no longer applicable. Suppose the staff members know more than their bosses, have a better feel for the market, and are closer to the customers. Suppose talking or writing is action and that the staff members value the approbation of their professional peers more than that of their leaders. Is it possible to "lead" such an organization? Not according to classical theory; it would be like herding cats. Yet that is precisely the kind of situation that the heads of tomorrow's organizational entities will have to confront. These entities have been labeled "fishnets" (Johansen and Swiegart 1994) and "networks" (Grenier and Metes 1992). They have been described as virtual (Davidow and Malone 1992), irrational (Brunsson 1985), three–dimensional (Czarniawska–Joerges 1993), hypertextual (Nonaka and Takeuchi 1995), adhocratic (Mintzberg 1979), intelligent (Quinn 1992, Pinchot and Pinchot 1995), transcendent (Gustavsson 1992), learning (Senge 1990), and imaginary (Hedberg 1995).

Yesterday's managers could rely on their workers' loyalty, which was born of necessity. Not so in the future. The operatives of knowledge organizations are highly educated knowledge workers (Drucker 1993) and reflective practitioners (Schön 1983). They are the "illoyal new individualists" (Leinberger and Tucker 1991), members of Generation X (Coupland 1991), who form a new elite. They keep well informed through their contacts with customers and vendors and through membership in informal networks in which knowledge flows freely and information is abundant.

Thus, production in future organizations is likely to be totally different from the production envisaged by classic theory, which occurs within the four walls of a factory and takes the form of the movement of tangible material through the stages of a concrete production process. Much of the future organizations' business will be done off-site in customers' offices or during private meetings to which company leaders will never be invited. They will not possibly be able to interact with all the networks or have access to all the sources of knowledge.

Do companies that are lean (Womack and Jones 1994), "nice" (Lloyd 1988), self-organizing (Jantsch 1980), or self-ruling (Wheatley 1995) really need managers? In fact, the answer seems to be yes, but they must learn how to dance (Moss-Kanter 1990) and thrive on chaos (Peters 1992) because they will manage on the edge (Pascal 1990). They must master the fifth discipline, that is, systemic thinking (Senge 1990). So they must communicate silently (Hall 1959) in teams that work on a global basis (Johansen et al. 1991) to reengineer (Hammer and Champy 1993) and implement total quality (Cullen and Hollingum 1987). If the managers succeed they are promised a new world of increasing returns (Arthur 1996).

This eclectic collection of concepts reflects the present confusion about the way we perceive the future world. There is good reason for the confusion.

▪ From Industry Paradigm to Knowledge Paradigm

There seems to be a fair amount of consensus about the old world; let's label it *the industrial paradigm*. Everyone agrees that we are leaving the industrial way of seeing the world, but no one can say with any certainty what will take its place. The new whatever-we-call-it appears to be intangible and chaotic, individual and global, small and big, machinelike and human, all at the same time. It seems reasonably clear, however, that information and knowledge, in the widest sense, are becoming more important. So however we describe the new society that we're creating, it makes sense to think of it in terms of knowledge.

We already live in a world in which services constitute more than two-thirds of both the gross national product (GNP) and employment, so we must shift our perspective—or the paradigm—to something that we can call a service or *knowledge economy* (Quinn 1992).

A paradigm shift (Kuhn 1962) takes place when a sufficient proportion of people change their way of seeing the world and begin seeing phenomena from a new shared perspective. A new paradigm is very difficult to "see" because most of us remain trapped by the language of the old paradigm while we struggle to define the new.[3]

Item	Seen with an industrial paradigm, or from an industrial perspective	Seen with a knowledge paradigm, or from a knowledge perspective
People	Cost generators or resources	Revenue generators
Managers' power base	Relative level in organization's hierarchy	Relative level of knowledge
Power struggle	Physical laborers versus capitalists	Knowledge workers versus managers
Main task of management	Supervising subordinates	Supporting colleagues
Information	Control instrument	Tool for communication, resource
Production	Physical laborers processing physical resources to create tangible products	Knowledge workers converting knowledge into intangible structures
Information flow	Via organizational hierarchy	Via collegial networks
Primary form of revenues	Tangible (money)	Intangible (learning, new ideas, new customers, R&D)
Production bottlenecks	Financial capital and human skills	Time and knowledge
Manifestation of production	Tangible products (hardware)	Intangible structures (concepts and software)
Production flow	Machine-driven, sequential	Idea-driven, chaotic
Effect of size	Economy of scale in production process	Economy of scope of networks
Customer relations	One way via markets	Interactive via personal networks
Knowledge	A tool or resource among others	The focus of business
Purpose of learning	Application of new tools	Creation of new assets
Stock market values	Driven by tangible assets	Driven by intangible assets
Economy	Of diminishing returns	Of both increasing and diminishing returns

Exhibit 2. The principles of the knowledge organization.

The label I have chosen for the new knowledge paradigm is *seeing the world from a knowledge perspective*. This description best fits the message of this book, but I am far from certain it will remain the best even five years from now. Exhibit 2 describes how I interpret what is happening. The right–hand column also summarizes the guiding principles for the organization that I have designed as an archetype for the future: *the knowledge organization.*

What are the practical management consequences of these sweeping principles? I believe that some of the answers can be found among the companies in the business services sector because many of them are already operating in the knowledge economy. For these companies, intangible assets are the most valuable assets.

Summary

- The economy of the knowledge era offers unlimited resources because the human capacity to create knowledge is infinite.
- Unlike physical resources, knowledge grows when it is shared. However, the distinction between organizations that sell derivatives of knowledge and those that sell knowledge as a process is vitally important because the art of achieving increasing returns is different for each. For the former, it is driven by information; for the latter, it is driven by knowledge.
- Human production can be seen as a creation of knowledge and distribution as a creation of knowledge together with customers.

Advice to Managers

- Managers often have an unconscious and tacit mindset that is colored by the values and the common sense of the industrial age. To see another world, they need to try to use a conscious mindset such as the knowledge perspective.
- It is best not to dress present–day experiences in words or concepts from the industrial era because then one fails to see the new. It is best to try to avoid the "mindtrap" of industrial society logic. The logic of the knowledge era seems in many ways to be the opposite of traditional industrial age logic.
- Currently available statistics do not clarify the very rapid expansion of knowledge companies in the service sector. It is important to try to find alternative statistical data.

What Is Knowledge?
What Is Competence?

Employee competence is not merely one of the three intangible assets of an organization, it is also the source of the organization's internal and external structures. Therefore, in order to manage and measure intangible assets, we need to understand what competence is. To gain that understanding, we must answer the question, "What is knowledge?"

This question has exercised the minds of philosophers over the ages, but no consensus—no generally accepted definition of the word—has been reached. The term *epistemology*—theory of knowledge—comes from the Greek word *episteme*, which means absolute certain truth. But in English, the word *knowledge* seems to be a multifaceted thing. It can mean information, awareness, knowing, cognition, sapience, cognizance, science, experience, skill, insight, competence, know-how, practical ability, capability, learning, wisdom, certainty, and so on. The definition depends on the context in which the term is used.[1]

I believe that knowledge has four characteristics.

Knowledge Is Tacit

The question of certainty is of little importance to managers, who have to operate in the real world where one can never be absolutely certain of anything. In contrast, practical knowledge is important to managers, but it is very difficult to express in words. How do you explain in words how to skate or serve a tennis ball? Practical knowledge is—to a very large extent—tacit.

Michael Polanyi developed his theory of tacit knowledge in the late 1940s and early 1950s. Polanyi lived at the time when information theory and cybernetics were born, and he illustrates his theories with examples from the scientific professions. These aspects of his work make him seem very modern today because the working conditions of scientists are quite similar to those of present–day knowledge workers involved in information processing.[2]

Polanyi regards knowledge as both personal, that is, formed in a social context, and individual, that is, not the property of an organization or a collective. His concept of knowledge is based on three main theses:

1. True discovery cannot be accounted for by a set of articulated rules or algorithms.
2. Knowledge is at the same time public and, to a great extent, personal (that is, because it is constructed by humans it contains emotions, or passion).
3. The knowledge that underlies explicit knowledge is the more fundamental; all knowledge is either tacit or rooted in tacit knowledge, that is, rooted in practice.

Thus, in Polanyi's world there is no such thing as objective knowledge in the scientific sense, no *episteme*, no absolute certainty. However, knowledge is not private or subjective. Although it is personal, it is also socially constructed. Socially conveyed knowledge blends with the individual's experience of reality. New experiences are always assimilated through the concepts that an individual possesses.[3]

Those concepts are tacit. Individuals change or adapt the concepts in the light of their experiences and reinterpret the language used to express them. When a new word or concept is brought into an older system of language, each affects the other. The system itself enriches what the individual has brought to it. All of our knowledge therefore has a tacit dimension.

Let me explain further. Any activity is accomplished through the use of two dimensions of knowledge: *focal knowledge* is the knowledge about the object or phenomenon that is in focus; *tacit knowledge* is the knowledge that is used as a tool to handle what is being focused on.

Tacit and focal knowledge are not categories or levels in a hierarchy but rather two dimensions of the same whole. They are complementary: tacit knowledge functions as background knowledge that assists in accomplishing the task that is in focus. Furthermore, the tacit part of knowledge varies from one situation to another. For instance, when reading a text, words and linguistic rules function as tacit or subsidiary knowledge while the reader's attention is focused on the meaning of the text. Polanyi offers another example: "When we use a hammer to drive a nail, we attend to both nail and hammer, but in a different way. . . . The difference may be stated by saying that the latter (hammers) are not like the nails, objects of our attention, but instruments of it. They are not watched in themselves; we watch something else while keeping intensely aware of them. I have a *subsidiary awareness* of the feeling in the palm of my hand which is merged into my *focal awareness* of my driving in the nail" (Polanyi 1958, 55).

Whether knowledge is used in a tacit or a focused way depends on the situation. Polanyi emphasizes the functional aspect of knowledge: unreflected knowledge is like a (tacit) tool by which we either act or gather new knowledge. The tool—like the hammer—is taken for granted.

⁌ Knowledge Is Action-Oriented

We are constantly generating new knowledge by analyzing the sensory impressions we receive (and the more senses we employ in the process, the better) and constantly losing old knowledge. This dynamic quality of knowledge is reflected in verbs like *learn, forget, remember,* and *understand.*

To describe how we acquire and create new knowledge by applying to our sensory inputs the abilities and facts we already possess, Michael Polanyi uses the term *process-of-knowing.* Inspired by Gestalt psychology, Polanyi regards the process-of-knowing as one of gathering fragmentary clues, through sensory perceptions and from memories, and integrating them under categories. In other words, we make sense of reality by categorizing it into theories, methods, feelings, values, and skills that we can use in a fashion that tradition judges to be valid.

We attend from the particulars to the focus upon which they bear. For example, we see part of an object or part of a set of data that reminds us of something with which we are familiar and we fill in the blanks. This act of integration is an informal act of the mind and cannot be accomplished by a formal operation or system of artificial intelligence. The integration of knowledge is a personal skill. It cannot be disposed of or transferred; each person must build it up individually.

Polanyi frequently uses the verb *know* and the noun *knowledge* synonymously. In his later work *(The Tacit Dimension,* 1967), he emphasizes the dynamic properties of knowledge. He even describes knowledge as an activity: "Knowledge is an activity that would be better described as a process-of-knowing."[4]

Here is an exercise that will help clarify the nature of tacit knowledge. Shut your eyes, then try to touch the tip of your nose with your index finger. Concentrate on where your arm is at all times. Take twenty seconds to do this exercise.

How did it go? Quite well, probably. You likely succeeded in touching the tip of your nose even though you could not see it. This is because you tacitly know where the tip of your nose is, and you know how you must move your arm and finger to touch it. You were consciously focusing on this knowledge.

We do not usually focus consciously on physical movements like this one; we would get little done if we did. Compared with our subconscious minds, our conscious minds are hopelessly inefficient information-processors. Recent studies (Nörretranders 1992) show that the conscious mind can process between sixteen and forty bits of information per second. But the subconscious mind can handle eleven million bits per second. In other words, we're aware of barely a millionth of the information that our brains process. While you were deliberately focusing on the movement of your arm, your brain was rapidly and efficiently dealing with the enormous amount of information needed to manage your body.

Conscious thought is energy-intensive and inefficient, but it is also very flexible. It can be switched consciously (or distracted unconsciously) in a fraction of a second—to concentrate attention on our heads or our toes, to listen carefully, to think reflectively.

ᴵ Knowledge Is Supported by Rules

There are also rules for consciously and unconsciously processing knowledge. Which hand did you use in the nose-touching exercise? If you are right-handed, you probably used your right hand. Why didn't you use your left hand? You probably never gave it a thought; your action was purely automatic.

Over the years we build up innumerable patterns in our brains that act like unconscious rules of procedure to cope with every conceivable situation. These rules save us a great deal of energy and enable us to act quickly and effectively without having to stop to think about what we are doing.

These procedural rules also play a vital role in acquiring and improving skills. When we practice an activity, we test these rules and try to refine them. Is my backhand more effective when I angle the racket a little more when accomplishing that stroke? Does the piano sound any better if I raise my hand a little higher when playing those notes?

Rules are tied to the result of actions. The knowledge of the rules also functions as a tacit knowledge, that is, as a kind of "tool of tools." A rule is a standard for correctness. Rules develop during the process-of-knowing or through tradition (that is, by doing). Mastery of the rules also brings with it the ability to change them or extend them. Although rules are generally tacit, they may be articulated into explicit rules of thumb.

Polanyi maintains that craftsmen (his term is *makers*) use the same kinds of methods as other practitioners (*doers*) and as *thinkers*. Thus, scientists and carpenters are alike. They both follow rules and models and rely on experience to make judgments. Polanyi makes no clear distinction between practical knowledge and other kinds of knowledge, such as theoretical knowledge. He therefore makes no difference in principle between the analytical skills of a Bertrand Russel and a blind man's ability to use a cane. For Polanyi, the process-of-knowing is the same.

But intellectual tools are different from physical tools because they are based in a social context; they are used in interactions with other people. To use intellectual tools, a person needs to be confident in the social context. This is an important distinction as regards the rules and the tools, particularly for professionals involved in information processing.

RULES ACT AS FILTERS FOR KNOWING

Although they are helpful, rules of procedure are also limiting because they filter new knowledge. If you used your right hand in the nose exercise earlier, you denied yourself the experience of doing it with your left hand. No great loss in this case, perhaps, but consider how you act in more complex situations. How much of what you do just happens automatically? How much of your ability to create new knowledge do you unconsciously switch off?

When we are tacitly involved in a process-of-knowing we act unconsciously, we do not reflect. This is how we take things for granted. Traces of what we once knew always remain. Once I learn to ride a bicycle or play the piano, I never forget these skills entirely. Even when we call up fragments of knowledge or rules of procedure to our conscious minds, tacit residues always remain in our unconscious minds, automatically coloring new experiences. Unlike computers, human beings can never forget everything. As John Maynard Keynes once said, "The greatest difficulty lies not in persuading people to accept new ideas, but in persuading them to abandon old ones."

Human beings probably evolved this brain pattern system in order to respond quickly—without wasting time and energy on conscious deliberation—to sudden threats in a generally hostile environment. These days, the physical environment is less hostile. Most of us spend more time acting and reacting mentally—writing, talking, thinking—than physically. So the focus of this aboriginal brain pattern system has switched to helping us perform mental tasks quickly. We use it in simple calculating tasks, like multiplying numbers by recalling tables we learned in childhood, and in complex social tasks that those who work in large organizations have to undertake everyday, like writing memos, making presentations, and deciding how to behave in meetings.

So we constantly and unconsciously adopt more or less fixed patterns and perceptions when we react to the world around us. They may take the form of value judgments and more or less conscious attitudes. If they are sufficiently rigid—if we "know," for example, how a manager "should" behave to succeed and that "money always motivates people"—we can use such category labeling to find our way quickly and easily through the world instead of asking questions, listening, and creating new knowledge. We can act much more quickly when we don't stop to reflect. But when we refrain in this way from conscious deliberation it is not clear if the actions we take are really appropriate or suitable.

꙳ Knowledge Is Constantly Changing

Polanyi sometimes describes knowledge as an object that can be articulated in words. When tacit knowledge is made explicit through language, it becomes static. It can then be focused on for reflection. By distancing the actor from the knowledge and articulating the knowledge in language or symbols, the knowledge can be distributed, critiqued, and thereby increased.

Because we always know more than we can tell, it follows that what has been articulated and formalized is less than what we tacitly know. Explicit knowledge in the form of facts is therefore—metaphorically speaking—only the tip of the iceberg. Language alone is not enough for making knowledge explicit.

All articulated theoretical knowledge was originally constructed in my mind or someone else's. Facts are thus personal rather than objective in a positivistic scientific sense. Facts can be tested for their truth by an act of assertion, but the act of assertion contains a tacit part too.[5]

This notion is supported by Wittgenstein (both in his early *Tractatus* and in his later *Philosophical Investigations*). Wittgenstein points out that the inexpressible exists, that intangible concepts like *play, sound, move,* and so on cannot be explained in words but only by showing. Hence his famous last proposition (7.0) in *Tractatus*: "Whereof one cannot speak, thereof one must be silent."

The same argument goes for a complex concept like knowledge: it cannot be expressed in words. Thus, Wittgenstein drew the inevitable conclusion: philosophers who tried to do so were wasting their time.

From Knowledge to Competence

Thus, human knowledge is tacit, it is action-oriented, it is based on rules, it is individual, and it is constantly changing. Because the word *knowledge* is a notion with so many connotations, it is often not practical to use it. Even if knowledge is dynamic, which is best described by a verb like *to know,* often a more practical description is a noun. In view of the attention the word *competence* has been attracting recently, it may be the best candidate in the English language.

An individual's competence can be regarded as consisting of five mutually dependent elements:

- *Explicit knowledge.* Explicit knowledge involves knowing facts. It is acquired mainly through information, often through formal education.
- *Skill.* This art of "knowing how" involves a practical proficiency—physical and mental—and is acquired mainly through training and practice. It includes knowledge of rules of procedure and communication skills.
- *Experience.* Experience is acquired mainly by reflecting on past mistakes and successes.
- *Value judgments.* Value judgments are perceptions of what the individual believes to be right. They act like conscious and unconscious filters for each individual's process-of-knowing.
- *Social network.* The social network is made up of the individual's relationships with other human beings in an environment and a culture that is transferred through tradition.

As the list implies, information (explicit knowledge) is only one element of competence. To a large extent, competence depends on the environment. This is particularly true of the experiential and social network components of competence. If a person moves to a new environment, he or she loses competence. For example, when a steel mill closes, furnace workers who were competent in the old environment lose the relationships maintained by the factory organization. Unless they find a similar organization, they cannot make use of their competence. When the work ethic is strong—as in the cultures that most of us belong to—these workers feel stripped of self-worth and lose self-esteem.

Thus, in the manufacturing industries, the workers' competence is closely linked to a particular physical environment—what I call the internal structure. They have few alternatives outside of it. In contrast, professionals build up competence tied to an independent network that is outside of any organization. This fact is one of the primary forces with which managers have to deal today.

Managerial competence too is contextual. Able managers rely heavily on their social network. Knowing what "triggers" certain individuals, what person to contact, which individuals to rely on, which people to be careful with—all of these are important social skills that to a large extent are linked to a particular organization. Thus when managers move to other companies, they too lose some of their competence. In other occupations, the social ability is less important. For example, sports, arts, and crafts emphasize skill (that is, knowing how). Great skill, whether in skiing, writing, or designing ceramics, takes time to develop.

Thus the term *competence*—used here as a synonym for both knowing and knowledge—is a much more comprehensive notion than the standard English connotation, which tends to confine itself to practical skill. Competence here is individual, and this concept is different from the general use of the term in organizational theory and strategy. Organizational theorists define competence as an organizational feature, as the link between knowledge and strategy, as the ability (the power) of an organization to act relative to other organizations. For example, Philip Selznick (1957) defines organizational competence as "distinctive competence," similar to the "competitive advantage" (Porter 1980) of an organization. Hamel and Prahalad (1990) build on the same tradition when they label the technical and managerial skills that enable an organization to survive as their "core competences."

▪ A Definition of Knowledge

Based on Michael Polanyi and Ludwig Wittgenstein, for the purposes of this book I define knowledge as *a capacity to act*. This is not an all-encompassing definition but rather a practical notion for managers to keep in mind as they read the rest of the book. One's capacity to act is created continuously by a process–of–knowing. In other words, it is contextual. Knowledge cannot be separated from its context. The notion also implies a teleological purpose. I believe that the human process–of–knowing is designed by nature to help us survive in an often hostile environment.

The "act" in the definition can be a practical one, like chopping wood and walking, or an intellectual one, like speaking and analyzing. In this book the dynamic and active properties of knowledge are emphasized, so the terms *knowledge, competence,* and *process-of-knowing* are all used. But as the word that best encompasses the aspects of practical knowledge, *competence* will be used.

▪ From Competence to Expertise

The more skilled we become, the more we can modify our rules of procedure. If we become highly skilled, we can even invent new rules, like the Swede Lofgren, who astonished the ski–jumping community by holding his skis in a V form instead of in the traditional parallel arrangement, or the American athlete Dick Fosbury, who began doing the high jump backwards. By rewriting the rules of their sports, Lofgren and Fosbury showed they were true experts. It is the same in every field of human endeavor, both intellectual and physical. The mark of a true expert is not the ability to recite and apply the rules but the confidence to break and replace them with better rules.

However, it is important to distinguish between rules of procedure that are exclusive to individuals and that enable them to walk, chop wood, or use a word processing program, for example, and rules of procedure that are assessed in collaboration with others. When one acquires an ability, one has learned to follow rules of procedure, like moving one's fingers in certain prescribed ways to coax music from a piano. But a person isn't competent until he or she has learned the whole framework of rules, has reviewed personal rules of procedure in the light of what others have achieved, and has been able to modify them. Only at this point can the individual focus his or her knowledge on the object and forget about the rules.

Let us say, for instance, that a person is competent in a foreign language. She may recall the meaning of a letter written to her but not the language in which it was written, even if I asked her about it while she was sitting with the letter folded in her lap. An individual is an expert when he is so highly skilled and familiar with everything relevant that others have done or said that he not only reviews and modifies his own rules but also develops new rules that are obviously better for everyone operating in his area of expertise.

It is difficult to transfer an ability from one person to another, but it is practically impossible to transfer expertise. An expert must build up his or her own expertise, create it from scratch. There are thus relatively few experts in each professional field. Expertise is power, because those who are known to possess it tend to influence how others think and to set the agenda for debate. (This will be discussed in Chapter 5.)

It is easy to forget how much of our world is the creation of experts because rules of procedure and concepts they develop survive them. Fosbury or Lofgren no longer personally exercise power over high jumping or ski jumping. The knowledge of experts diffuses until it eventually becomes common sense, that is, we all take it for granted and cease to see it. Their personal power has dissipated because it has become the framework for further knowledge creation.

Just as competence is the basis of each of the three intangible assets—as will be discussed in Chapter 5—the masters of competence (the experts) are the key players in the knowledge organization. Before we go further into this issue, however, we must move on to another part of the discussion of knowledge—how it is transferred. This subject is covered in Chapter 4.

Summary

- Knowledge is *a capacity to act.*
- Knowledge cannot be described in words because it is mainly tacit; we always know more than we can say. Knowledge is also both dynamic and static.
- The concept of *competence*, which embraces factual knowledge, skill, experience, value judgments, and social networks, is the best way to describe knowledge in the business context.

▪ Practical knowledge is based on rules that do not change easily. Rules support the process–of–knowing but also restrict it. They allow us to act quickly but also tend to let us take things for granted.

▪ New knowledge is always colored by the knowledge we already possess. We can articulate or communicate parts of our knowledge so that it can be responded to.

▪ Explicit knowledge is independent of the individual that created it, but competence is not.

▪ Human competence cannot be copied exactly. We all develop our own competence—through training, practice, mistakes, reflection, and repetition. Competence is transferred by doing.

▪ Human knowledge can be seen as a sort of hierarchy with ability at the bottom (being most common), competence next, and expertise at the top (being most rare). Expertise is impossible to transfer. The power of expertise lies in the way that it influences how others think and behave.

The Key Activity in
Knowledge Organizations:
Transferring Knowledge

Competence, the most important of intangible assets, can be transferred from person to person in two different ways: through information or through tradition (that is, through doing). In order to manage competence, we must understand the best way to transfer it.

But first, an important distinction that was touched on in Chapter 3 must be made more explicit. That is, knowledge and information are different. Thinking of them as similar or synonymous distorts the entire concept of managing intangible assets.

◆ What Is Information?
When we speak or write, we use language to articulate some of our tacit knowledge in an attempt to pass it on to others. The name I give to these communications is *information*. Knowledge and information are often confused with each other. In the information technology industry, they are even used as synonyms. Thus, the word information is usually associated with both facts and the communication of facts.

Information is in many ways ideal for communicating explicit knowledge. It is fast, independent of the originator, and secure. All three of these features are of vital importance in the information technology era because the computer is designed to handle information. So it is tempting and seems commonsensical for the sender or speaker to attribute information with some sort of meaning.

The trouble is that people know more than they are conscious of or can put into words. For example, try to explain in words how to drive a golf ball or serve a tennis ball. These concepts are too complex to express fully in words. Attempts to do so are often ridiculous and almost always incomprehensible.

It is just as hard to explain through words alone what we do when we perform intellectual tasks, like speaking a foreign language, writing a memo, calculating the median of a series of numbers, or reading a graph. We learn the rules of procedure for doing these things in the same way that we learn to swim or ride a bike—through a combination of information, imitation, and most of all, practice.

People do not have to send signals to convey decipherable messages. An absent daughter who promised to phone during the weekend if she does not feel well sends a message by not phoning. Acquaintances who pass in the street without acknowledging each other transmit far more information than if they had exchanged greetings. We use our bodies as communication systems. Many studies have shown that a speaker's body language conveys up to three times as much meaning as his or her words.

PRACTICE: THE EMOTION THAT'S IN A WORD

Consider the three words *knowledge, information,* and *power,* and ask yourself what kind of associations—positive or negative—they bring to mind. Of the Americans and Europeans whom I have asked to try this exercise, almost all have reacted positively to the word *knowledge.* Some 50 percent to 60 percent reacted positively to *information,* but barely 10 percent reacted positively to *power.*

Yet none of these words are inherently positive or negative. They are just symbols. People react to them in particular ways because they bring their own meanings, emotions, and interpretations to the words in the light of past experiences in which they have heard the words used. All interpretation of information is based on experience, context, and situations and is colored by emotions. Thus, each interpretation is unique to each individual. My meaning can never be the same as yours, although it can come close. Close-knit communities, like families or small organizations, develop some metaphors and words with meaning for themselves only.

Thus, information is an unreliable and inefficient method for transferring knowledge from person to person because the receivers—not the senders—give the information its meaning. The meaning that one person expresses is never the same as the meaning generated in the mind of the person who receives it. Isn't it therefore more correct to regard information as meaningless?

SHANNON'S MEANINGLESS INFORMATION

In addition to the definitions of the word *information* as facts and the communication of facts, a third definition of the word is used in information theory and computer science, that is, *no meaning*. Claude Shannon of Bell Telephone, the inventor of the bit (a binary digit) and the byte (eight bits), defined information as a quantity of data carried by a telephone network. Shannon's concept is purely technical. It says nothing about the content or meaning of the information. He was interested in whether an "A" sent is an "A" received. This is why his ideas fit computers so well. Computer files contain nothing but bits. It is software that arranges them into words or images, on a screen or on paper, that can be interpreted by human beings.

Thus we have two distinct phenomena: *information,* in the form of numbers, symbols, pictures, or words displayed on a screen, and *knowledge,* which is what information becomes when it is interpreted. To a human interpreter, an "A" sent may be perceived as an "A," as an apple, as a grade, or as a picture of a plough as seen from above. A word or a character can evoke a wide range of associations depending on the context and the interpreter's experience and emotional state. Again, one person's interpretation is never quite the same as another's.

When Alan Turing and Norbert Wiener developed their mathematical models for the computer in the 1940s, they assumed they were emulating the human brain. They and many of their contemporaries believed that systems science and information theory closely mirrored the way human beings acquire knowledge. In fact, information theory functions admirably when applied to communication between computers, but we have known since the 1970s that our brains operate according to very different principles. What we call *knowledge* is derived from processes that are vastly more complex than those available to the information technology industry.

Shannon's mathematical formula for information is the same as entropy, that is, chaos. Shannon himself initially wanted to use the word entropy instead of information. In his formula more entropy equals more information, so one conclusion from the theory is that there is more information in chaos than in structure, an idea that seems to go against common sense. Shannon's idea that information is chaotic, however, fits remarkably well with the seemingly nonsensible behavior of the information markets. (Chapter 7 discusses this issue in greater depth.)

ıˑ A Radical Notion of Information

In today's chaotic information markets, a report with lots of figures is refuted the following week by another report on the same subject that has very different figures. The facts from one database tell one story while the facts from a second database tell another. A report predicting disaster is contradicted by a more sanguine forecast. The contradictions occur sometimes because of errors in analysis but more often because reality is contradictory.

Is a chaos of information better than none at all? When you can pick and choose information, there is always some authority that will support a particular view. How often do managers assemble and present information simply to validate decisions they have made on other grounds? There is more wisdom in one experienced manager's "gut feeling" than in any amount of information to be found in databases or books. Information does not solve the age-old problem of how to orient ourselves in, and cope with, the chaos we call the world. On the contrary, the evidence from what I term *the informatized markets* suggests that we should turn our concept of information on its head and acknowledge the following radical notion: *information is meaningless and of low value.*

Thus, the concept of information is fuzzy, but given the choice between the commonsensical notion of it and the radical notion of it, I lean toward the radical. I believe that adopting such a radical notion will prepare us far better for the future and save companies and governments money and their employees and citizens pain.

Currently, however, governments and many businesses alike act as if information is meaningful and has a high value. The European Union is even trying to devise a legal copyright framework based on that notion. Yet the value does not lie in the information stored but in the knowledge creation that it may be part of. Knowledge creation from information is a heavy investment; the value of information itself pales in comparison.

ıˑ Knowledge Transfer via Tradition

Numerous attempts have been made to measure the effectiveness of the various methods of transferring competence. They show that the most common method—the lecture—is also the least effective. After five days, most people remember less than a tenth of what they heard during a lecture. A combination of seeing and hearing is somewhat better, with a retention of about 20 percent. But learning by doing is most effective: people remember 60 percent to 70 percent of what they do. Lectures and audiovisual presentations are examples of knowledge transfer by information; learning by doing is an example of knowledge transfer by tradition.

If the objective is to enhance competence, knowledge transfer via information is not a reliable transfer method; one needs more osmotic methods that resemble the traditional passing down of knowledge from master to apprentice.

Modern information technology is adept at transmitting and copying information at high speed from computer to computer. But people learn mainly by following each other's example, by practicing, and by talking. We dislike reading and interpreting instructions. Who among us over the age of twenty-five can program a VCR to record automatically? The instruction manual tends to be so incomprehensible that it merely confuses, so we don't bother to open it. Computer hackers are no different; indeed, an axiom among computer hackers is "When all else fails read the manual!"

People generally prefer to "discover" knowledge by experimenting. Most of us don't begin by reading manuals any more than we endeavor to become better corporate executives by interpreting information in a book about management like this one. The most books can provide the reader with is a framework for interpretation that can then be tested by acting on it.

Thus, competence is transferred most effectively when the recipient participates in the process. Since time immemorial, craftsmen have transferred (handed down or "traded" in the original sense of the word) their skills through master–apprentice relationships. The masters show how things are done, the apprentices try to imitate them, and the masters judge their efforts. Gradually, the apprentices learn to apply the rules themselves and become more proficient. They start looking elsewhere for inspiration, and they find other masters and learn from the vast accumulation of knowledge in libraries or other experts. Eventually, they may become so skillful that they make themselves independent of their masters and write their own rules. In other words, they become experts. It is this process that Michael Polanyi calls tradition: the process in which the apprentice personally re-creates the master's skills.

Furthermore, an individual's room for improvement is infinite. When an old master like director Ingmar Bergman reminisces, he wryly recalls his early efforts at film and theater. He says that his first few years in the profession were really just an apprenticeship and that he is still always learning something new. The memoirs of artists and other illustrious people always include tributes to early men-tors—experienced professionals who took them in hand. It was from such people and during such occasions that Ingmar Bergman learned his most important lessons, albeit on an ad hoc basis.

Similarly, the skills of leadership cannot be learned except through practice. No one can become a master without first having been an apprentice. One can't become a world champion swimmer without getting more than one's feet wet. This kind of learning by doing occurs in all professions, and the rules are more or less uni-versal. Tradition extends beyond organizations and nations. Tradition enables professionals to talk to each other and so transfer knowledge effectively. Even during the cold war, Russian and American doctors felt at home with each other and could talk easily. Journalists too have rules of thumb for the development and presentation of an article that are much the same everywhere. Every major city has some kind of press club where journalists of all nationalities can socialize. Pro-fessionals tend to club together in associations where they can meet people from whom they can learn. This kind of socializing has prob-ably been going on since the dawn of human history. It was already

Information	Tradition
Transfers articulated information	Transfers unarticulated and articulated abilities
Independent of the individual	Dependent and independent
Static	Dynamic
Quick	Slow
Codified	Uncodified
Easy mass distribution	Difficult mass distribution

Exhibit 3. The transfer of knowledge takes place in two main ways: through information and through tradition.

developed in the Middle Ages when associations of painters and comb makers, for example, formed guilds in Europe, many of which still survived long after the crafts they represent became redundant. The modern equivalents are the accountant institutes, the medical associations, the law societies. Tradition remains the best way to transfer competence. We know that on-the-job learning is the best form of learning in the workplace.

But learning by tradition takes time, and time is a commodity that we seem to have less and less of, even though people now live longer than ever before. Another drawback to tradition is that so much of it is tacit that one often has to be part of a profession to acquire its skills. Exhibit 3 summarizes the characteristics of learning through information and of learning through tradition.

Although tradition is slower than information at transferring facts, it is a very effective way to transfer competence because it makes use of all the senses, including the sixth sense. Textbooks and formal lessons are not needed. It is often enough to work alongside someone who knows more than you do to learn from her. The transfer occurs automatically and unconsciously. When working within a tradition, we learn so much that we are unaware of how much we know; remember the term *tacit knowledge*, explained in Chapter 3.

The trouble with tacit knowledge, or tacit knowing, is that because it lives in the unconscious, it often operates as a constraint, as in the nose-touching exercise described in Chapter 3. We see what we have learned to see. Thus, experts tend to have one-track minds. Lawyers assume that there are legal solutions to every problem; economists think all problems are economic. This is why, as Exhibit 3 implies, it is valuable to have an interaction between information and tradition, between explicit and tacit knowledge.

ꞏꞏ Knowledge Creation

The concept that knowledge is created by an interaction of the two types of knowledge—explicit and tacit—was suggested by Nonaka and Takeuchi (*The Knowledge-Creating Company*, 1995). In that work, which is likely to become a classic in the field, Nonaka and Takeuchi explain how Japanese companies during the 1980s innovated by a process of interaction between explicit and tacit knowledge.

The authors claim that at the heart of successful Japanese companies lies an understanding of knowledge that sees body and mind as a whole. They point out that most Western thinkers, in contrast, are caught in the Cartesian dualism that mind and body are different. Polanyi is one of the few Western philosophers to emphasize the bodily experience in learning and the involvement of the knower in everything known. Nonaka and Takeuchi rightly criticize Western management and organization theorists for being preoccupied with "the acquisition, accumulation, and utilization of existing knowledge; they lack the perspective of creating new knowledge" (1995, 49). In particular they argue against those organizational learning theorists who, based on Argyris and Schön (1978), argue that organizations can manage "single-loop learning" themselves but that "double-loop learning" requires outside intervention. A knowledge-creating company, they say, is able to change its fundamental rules too by an interaction between tacit and explicit knowledge.

This interaction is the authors' core concept. By *tacit knowledge*, they refer to the knowledge of the body, which is subjective, practical, analog. By *explicit knowledge*, they refer to the knowledge of the mind, which is objective, theoretical, digital. The interaction of tacit and explicit knowledge they call *process knowledge conversion*.

The authors show how Japanese manufacturing companies during the 1980s used four processes of knowledge conversion to design new and creative products. These processes are shown in Figure 8. They are *socialization*, *externalization*, *internalization*, and *combination*.

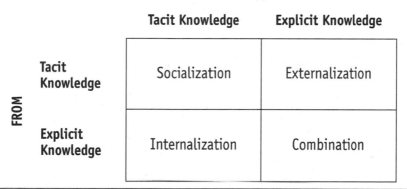

Figure 8. *Four modes of knowledge conversion.*

Socialization is a process of sharing experience and thereby creating tacit knowledge, such as shared mental models and skills. For example, when apprentices work with their masters they learn craftsmanship through observation, imitation, and practice. Language is not sufficient.

Externalization is a process of articulating tacit knowledge into explicit concepts. In spoken words, the tacit knowledge takes the form of metaphors, models, concepts, and equations, which express in a reduced and somewhat distorted form the tacit knowledge of an individual. Management books are examples of externalization.

Combination is the process of systemizing explicit concepts into a knowledge system, that is, combining different bodies of explicit knowledge into new explicit knowledge by analyzing, categorizing, and reconfiguring information. This form of knowledge conversion takes place in universities and other formal education forums. Databases and computer networks are the new tools for this kind of knowledge conversion. The Intangible Assets Monitor described in Chapter 13 is an example of how a combination of many data sources into a new format can yield new insights.

Internalization refers to the absorption of explicit knowledge into tacit knowledge. It is closely related to learning by doing. Internalization is helped along if the knowledge is verbalized as oral stories or if systems document processes are used. Simulations are another way to accomplish this mode of knowledge conversion to improve knowledge creation. (See Chapter 8 for more on simulations.) Chapter 7 will show how these four processes can help in the management of the internal structure of an organization.

Nonaka and Takeuchi's concepts are similar in many ways to mine. Their idea of interaction between explicit and tacit knowledge is a powerful metaphor for managers in product development. The four modes of knowledge conversion can be used to shed light on the production process of professionals working in knowledge organizations. In *The Knowledge-Creating Company*, they describe the internal innovation processes of three Japanese manufacturing companies, processes that are similar to the "production" that the knowledge workers of my "knowledge organization" accomplish when they work with customers.

▪▪ Two Traditions: Professional and Organizational

Transferring knowledge by doing within a knowledge organization involves two distinct traditions: the professional (or expert) tradition described in the previous section, where the professional is the vehicle of the tradition, and the organizational tradition, where the manager conveys the knowledge.

The tradition of organizational knowledge is similar to that of professional knowledge discussed earlier but not as strong. For instance, representatives of the former do not form guilds. Organizational knowledge is transferred by managers when they move between organizations and via the curriculum of management and business schools as well as through books by academic authors and management consultants.

It is useful to make the distinction between the professional and the organizational traditions because in this way the professionals and the managers become members of two different traditions. The main difference is probably that organizational competence has to do with how to influence the ways in which other people use their competence. The main task of managers is to lead activities with the help of others. They are often heads of functional areas. During their careers, professionals and managers therefore tend to develop their competencies along different paths, unless urged not to.

Managers and professionals generally have different responsibilities in organizations and, in many companies, even different remuneration systems, which stress their differences further. The differences between the two are also emphasized by business school curricula that still favor management of manufacturing companies with little emphasis given to management of knowledge organizations and knowledge professionals. Managers and professionals therefore often find themselves involved in bitter power plays. In some industries—the media industry, for example—they have dug particularly deep trenches. The power play between editors and managers can be quite heated.

Thus, professionals and managers not only represent the two ways of transferring knowledge by tradition but also are two of the power players in a knowledge organization. In the next chapter, I discuss the characteristics of professionals and managers in more detail and elaborate on the implications of their differences to the organization.

Summary

- Knowledge can be transferred in two ways. *Information* transfers knowledge indirectly through media such as lectures and audiovisual presentations; *tradition* transfers knowledge directly, from person to person, through learning by doing.
- Information and knowledge should be seen as distinctly different. Information is entropic (chaotic); knowledge is nonentropic. The receiver of information—not the sender—gives it meaning. Information, as such, is meaningless. Information is perfect for

broadcasting articulated knowledge but is unreliable and inefficient for transferring knowledge from person to person. Tradition should be used to transfer knowledge. Games, simulation models, and role-playing are all good because they resemble traditional learning methods, in which the student personally re-creates the teacher's skills.

- To use a computer-based metaphor, facts might be considered digital while skills might be considered analog.

Advice to Managers

- Information is meaningless and of low value.
- Information should be treated as a glut product with little or no economic value.
- Tacit knowledge that is articulated as information ages rapidly.
- The power of information is vanishing in the developed countries.
- People learn best by using their whole bodies. Games, simulation models, and role-playing are good ways to transfer knowledge.
- It is best not to write but to talk when we wish to transfer knowledge.

2

Managing
Intangible Assets

Managing
Intangible Assets

This section begins with Chapter 5, which describes the cast of characters in the knowledge organization—the four power players who together create intangible assets. Their characteristics and personal agendas must be understood before these assets can be managed effectively.

Chapters 6 through 10 discuss how to manage competence; how to manage the internal structure, with one chapter each about the operational and strategic aspects of doing so; and how to manage the external structure, with one chapter describing the two possible strategies—a knowledge-focused strategy and an information-focused strategy—and a second comparing the two strategies.

The Four Power Players
in the Knowledge Organization

When a company consists largely of skilled professionals who use their creativity to solve complex problems for its customers, that company operates in a special way, a way that reflects the forces influencing and controlling the organization. These same forces are in effect in all organizations that employ highly skilled people. The strength of the forces increases the closer one gets to the archetypal knowledge organization—the consulting firm. Such firms function in similar ways regardless of whether they're in the public or private sector.

Many supposed "leaders" fondly imagine that they are running their organizations when all they are doing is allowing them to run themselves. They do not understand the power play at work and are measuring the wrong things. As mentioned in Chapter 4, the power struggle within a knowledge organization generally occurs between representatives from the two knowledge traditions: the professional and the organizational. These two traditions form the vertical and horizontal axes of Figure 9. Within this framework, the organization employs four major players: the professional, the manager, the support staff, and the leader.

Understanding the agendas of these four players can point the way to managing an organization successfully or demonstrate how an organization will function if left unmanaged. Let us begin our analysis of the four players with the star: the professional.

Organizational Competence

The Professional	The Leader
The Support Staff	The Manager

Professional Competence (left vertical axis label)

Figure 9. The four personnel categories in knowledge organizations.

◢ The Professional

The professionals are the specialists, the authorities—whatever they may be called in a specific organization. Among this corps of professionals, the elite are the experts—and you can't miss them. Here is a snapshot picture of this personality type:

The expert strolls in past the reception desk in the morning without giving the receptionist a glance; he does not remember her name. He walks, not to his own office, but to that of another top professional. A lively debate ensues. There is much laughter, then a quick foray to the kitchen for cups of coffee. The door closes again; there are more loud voices, more volleys of laughter. Someone rushes out, grabs a document, rushes back. There is lots of activity on the other side of the door.

The receptionist gazes sadly at the closed door and sighs. "A normal morning," she thinks. "Everyone is having fun except me."

The expert and the mentor emerge, both wearing broad grins. They have just solved an important problem for a customer. It was that problem that had been occupying the expert's mind when he walked through the door that morning. He had been thinking about it all night; he didn't get a wink of sleep. The answer had come to him in the morning. That was why he ignored the receptionist. He was totally preoccupied with the problem and his elegant solution. Nothing mattered except what his colleague thought of the idea and whether he held the last pieces needed to complete the puzzle.

As this anecdote suggests, elite professionals share three primary characteristics.

A FOCUS ON THE JOB

"You concentrate so hard when you get out on the rink, it's as if you had a wall around you. You don't think about the spectators, just about what you've got to do," says Thomas Gradin, a National Hockey League player.

Similarly, experts focus on their jobs and their professions. Everything else is subordinate to the task at hand: finding a solution to the problem. On another day, the previously described ill-mannered expert might not come to the office at all because the answer to a problem will lie outside it, with a friend in another firm, in a library, or maybe at home through a couple of hours' contemplation or interfacing with a PC.

Naturally, our ill-mannered expert will forget to call the office to say he will not be coming in. So the receptionists who take his calls will not know what to say. And experts receive lots of calls, for they are widely respected outside the firm. When customers call, it is the expert to whom they want to talk, not the CEO. The expert is in demand as a speaker at symposia and has contacts with professional colleagues all over the world.

In short, the experts are the leading lights in their professions, highly intelligent and creative people. But they are often hopeless at planning their time, lack even a smidgen of administrative ability, have no sense of time and place, and are perceived as rude to those whom they regard as ignorant. Sometimes their supreme self-assurance comes over as sheer arrogance—for example, when the head of the accounting department asks about the holiday roster or the chargeable time for the past week and our expert snarls, "It isn't the time the job takes that matters, it's the result!" Experts are blithely unaware of the frustration they cause in those around them when they ignore matters crucial to the proper functioning of the organization.

As Figure 9 shows, professionals are high in professional competence, but low in organizational competence. The experts are even more pronounced in these directions.

PROFESSIONAL PRIDE

Self-assured, skilled professionals can be found in all walks of life: lawyers, police officers, physicians, art directors, architects, strategy consultants, computer programmers, cost accountants, electronic engineers. They're equally common in the craft trades, many of whom enjoy the status of respected experts in plumbing, painting, carpentry, and so on.

Skilled people tend to organize themselves in professional associations and to see themselves as upholders of their trade (the law, for example) or guardians (of freedom or of the language, for example) with a duty to protect their profession from attack and to maintain ethics standards.

Professions also subdivide themselves. The medical profession includes hundreds of different specialists. This kind of subdivision often results in heated territorial disputes and battles to secure resources for individual specialist areas. One of the least attractive habits of the professional bodies is their constant effort to restrict recruitment to their own fields in order to preserve their scarcity. They have been doing this since the medieval guilds, from which both unions and professional associations evolved.

The behavior of experts is so familiar and natural that even those who are not experts copy it. A survey of physicians in England found that medical students start acting like doctors as soon as their applications for medical school are accepted!

A DISLIKE OF ROUTINE

What professionals enjoy most is coming to grips with a thorny problem, whether it be an intricate electrical wiring system, a sophisticated roofing structure, a complicated process of reorganization, a challenging problem of communications, or a difficult diagnosis. What they enjoy least is solving a problem in the same way as last time.

In their constant effort to escape the drudgery of routine, professionals surround themselves with assistants. In the research laboratory, for example, test-tube shaking is delegated to the "lower" occupational category of laboratory technician. It goes without saying that senior research scientists, consultants, and law firm partners all need secretaries. Professionals are endlessly ingenious in finding rational arguments for this kind of vertical division of labor: assistants are cheaper, they leave professionals free to concentrate on more vital tasks, and so on. The problem is, this stratifies the organization, causing needless conflicts. Furthermore, assistants require direction—and if there is anything professionals are bad at, it is managing other people—and so this creates another source of potential conflict. The modest gains of delegation are thus often consumed by energy-intensive conflicts of interest and administration.

A SUMMARY OF CHARACTERISTICS

Now to summarize my portrait of experts:

- Experts like complex problems, new advances in their profession, freedom to seek solutions, well-equipped and funded laboratories, and public recognition of their achievements.
- Experts dislike rules limiting their individual freedom, routine work, and bureaucracy (which they tend to see everywhere).
- Experts care little about such things as pay, time off, the organization that employs them, and people who are ignorant of their specialization.
- Experts can seldom work through other people or lead an organization.
- Experts admire people more expert than themselves.
- Experts despise power-oriented people (that is, traditional bosses).

Happily, of course, few professionals, or even experts, truly resemble this caricature. Many doctors are caring and humane, many chimney sweeps clean the floor when they have finished with the chimney, plenty of experts in areas like finance and law are conspicuously generous. But although this caricature of the expert is mercifully rare in real life, most experts *do* display some of these characteristics. It is essential for leaders of companies who employ professionals to be on the lookout for them. For it is these professionals, with their distinctive qualities and motivations, who determine how a company dominated by professionals or creative people will behave when it lacks the right kind of leadership.

The Manager

Accountants are professionals; in an accounting firm they may be considered experts, but if they are business managers in law or architecture firms, their primary purpose is to manage. The same is true of the attorney who heads the human resource department of an organization rather than practices law in a law firm or of the person with a degree in systems theory who heads an accounting department rather than works for a software company. Thus, I define managers as people appointed by superiors to lead an organization toward a defined goal within a given frame of reference and specified resources. Their role is constrained within the parameters defined by a higher authority. Figure 9 shows them to be low in professional competence—that is, the competence of the knowledge organization—but high in organizational competence.

In many ways managers are the opposite of professionals as I use the term in this book. Whereas professionals work solely with customers and other professionals using their professional competence, managers use their organizational competence to oversee the work of others. They are capable of managing and organizing. They have learned to work through people, and they enjoy working with different sorts of people. Their main task is to lead activities with the help of others.

The team manager or project manager role is a very important one in knowledge organizations, but usually the team managers are experts and they tend to regard their leadership role as ancillary to their professional function. This contrasts with traditional industrial managers who run functional departments, sections, or groups. You find such managers everywhere in industry and civil service, but in knowledge organizations people who are simply functional managers are relatively scarce.

This playing down of the functional manager role is a fundamental difference between the traditional manufacturing company and the knowledge organization. For example, the financial controller of a knowledge organization tends to be the only member of his or her profession in the place, and thus he or she has no fellow professionals to share thoughts with. In private-sector knowledge organizations, moreover, the controllers are often the only upholders of "law and order," which means they frequently come into conflict with the organization's true professionals. They know little about the knowledge organization's business idea, and the knowledge organization's professionals know little about performance measuring or administration—and care even less about them—because they are totally focused on their own professions.

In leaderless knowledge organizations, the accounting function is given a low status, and the controllers tend to be isolated downward because of their police function and ignored upward because their methodology is that of the manufacturing company and thus measures only the "tip of the iceberg" as far as the knowledge organization is concerned. In leaderless knowledge organizations that are dominated by the values of the experts, the only option for the controllers—or any other functional managers—is often to leave the company and go to work for a larger industrial organization in which their skills are more valued.

▪▪ The Support Staff

The support staff is made up of the bookkeepers, personal assistants, secretaries, receptionists, and switchboard operators. Compared with the professionals, the support staff knows little about advertising, law, architecture, or whatever the organization's business idea may be. Their function is to assist professionals and managers. They have no special qualifications of their own to give them status in the knowledge organization. Figure 9 shows them to be low in both professional and organizational competence.

A well-motivated and qualified support staff is essential for the efficiency of an organization and its professionals. These people are essential in providing customers with an appropriate level of service. They are also an important element of the "glue" that gives the knowledge organization a modicum of law and order. But in a leaderless knowledge organization, however skillful a typist or good letter editor a secretary, he or she is not properly appreciated because the only knowledge that counts is knowledge relevant to the business idea. The situation is very different if the secretary works for an agency where secretarial skills are integral to the business idea. Experienced secretaries in such firms belong in the professional square of the organizational matrix.

But support staff in leaderless knowledge companies have to put up with bad bosses—perhaps former experts who don't take their management functions seriously or are not qualified to perform them, or perhaps discontented financial controllers who themselves feel left out of things.

How do people who work for incompetent managers in companies that do not appreciate them behave? How will the receptionist in the little tale told earlier in this chapter react? She will probably get together with the other support staff, join in groups of malcontents, and develop what may be called underdog symptoms. The support staff are usually the only ones who take regular coffee breaks—a quarter of an hour each morning and afternoon during which shop talk is banned.

Support staff often make modest demands. "We want ergonomic chairs." "We need radiation filters for our computer screens." "Nobody ever tells us anything." "Why can't we have an in-house bulletin?" Even in well-managed knowledge companies such complaints are often justified. The support staff is indeed the least well-informed group in the organization, not because of any ill will on the part of the experts or deliberate attempts to exclude them, but—as was discussed in Chapter 4—simply because informing people is such an inefficient way of communicating knowledge.

The real exchanges of information occur in conference rooms and in corridors in a language only the initiated understand. When two architects meet in a corridor, a thumbs-up gesture is enough for one to let the other know that the order they talked about earlier has been won. The gesture will trigger a number of connotations in the mind of the colleague, like "If we clinched the deal, I will have to reschedule tomorrow's work plan," or "Oh, I never believed we would do it because we were competing against X Company and they are so strong in this field. I wonder if we priced it too low," or "Our competitiveness must have improved!"

But the gesture means nothing to the receptionist who was not privy to the previous dialogue. Both the receptionist and professional were given the same message, but only one is informed by it. For the receptionist to understand the full implications of the gesture, the professional would have to give a lengthy explanation of what went on behind closed doors, and that would take too much time.

Years of mismanagement in the support staff area have left a potential for improvement in many companies.

ꞏꞏ The Leader

Leaders in successful knowledge organizations are high in both professional and organizational competence, not just in one or the other as are professionals and managers, as Figure 9 shows.

Leaders are usually former experts themselves. They belong to the same profession as the experts, but they need not be outstanding professionals. For example, in an orchestra the conductor is seldom a virtuoso on any instrument; in the theater the director may not be a great actor. Still, professional competence is essential if the leader is to bring out the best in the performers. In a knowledge organization such as a law or architectural firm, an accountant may be the business manager (as discussed earlier) and considered a manager. But the law firm's managing partner has a law degree and the architectural firm's managing partner has an architectural degree, and they will be considered leaders if they also are good at management and organization.

Leadership involves two tasks: knowing where one wants to go and persuading other people to go along. The first task requires analysis of options and an ability to form a concrete picture of the goal, often called *a vision*. The second task requires rare communicative ability, empathy, and energy. Asea Brown Boveri's (ABB) chief executive, Percy Barnevik, claims the first takes up 5 percent to 10 percent of his time and the second takes up the rest.

I believe altruism is another integral part of the leadership personality. A good leader's desire to lead springs from a desire to better the lot of those who are led. Leadership also implies movement (guiding groups of people in particular directions), and thus change. The following puts it simply:

- A leader changes, a manager preserves.
- Many managers are leaders, but most probably are not.
- Leaders are important people in a knowledge organization, and there are often more than one.

A leader must be motivated by a genuine desire to lead, inspired by a vision of where the organization is heading, able to unite people in the effort to realize the vision, totally committed to his or her task, and action-oriented.

Can leaders, no matter how talented, manage experts? I believe that the answer is yes. Granted, experts are often creative personalities, with all that that implies about them and those around them. Such people are not easygoing, uncontroversial types; that is not the nature of the creative personality. It is hardly their fault if they do not fit into molds that were not made for them; perhaps the fault lies not in them but in the molds.

One thing is abundantly clear, however: they do not make life easy for leaders. Theatrical directors, for example, are always accusing actors of being neurotic, stupid, impossible to deal with, complicated, egotistical, insecure, or just plain weird. But they say good things, too, about actors, that they have strong personalities, independence of mind, and artistic creativity, for example. Musicians are often said to be unbalanced and to have childish personalities, but they are also proud and self-assured. When musical and theatrical directors speak of musicians and actors, they seem to be speaking about willful children that they both love and detest. They regard this as quite natural, make allowances for it, and take advantage of it when exercising their leadership.

There are those who say creative people can't be led, that it is impossible to manage companies composed of insufferably egotistical, self-assured people who do not know the meaning of the word loyalty. Nevertheless, such companies *must* be led if they are to move in intended directions and not align themselves—much like compass needles—within the force fields that all knowledge organizations spontaneously generate.

Leadership in a knowledge organization is largely a matter of giving the experts creative freedom within a framework devised by the leader. To do that, the leader must, of course, know enough about the field or fields of specialization to be equipped to judge performance in relation to the framework. The art of leading knowledge organizations, therefore, is the art of handling professionals, particularly the experts, and the task of leadership in such organizations is to provide the professionals with conditions under which they can exercise their creativity for the benefit of customers while not letting the organization become entirely dependent on them.

Furthermore, leaders who are not initiates of the profession are at the mercy of the key people and powerless to get them to do anything they do not agree with. In a knowledge company with a leader not accepted by the experts, the internal forces are given free rein; the firm spontaneously aligns itself in accordance with its own internal power structure. In other words, the experts assume control. The result is that the official executives spend their time attending "important meetings," where they make equally important "decisions," while the rest of the company carries on, regardless. The leaderless company speedily becomes not only inefficient but, as my stereotypical expert's behavior displays, a terrible and neurotic place for most people to work in. A leaderless knowledge organization can often be identified by the degree of negative strains in the culture, as exemplified by the exodus of managers or a disgruntled support staff.

If an organization has no customers—either because it's an in-house department of a large organization or because, like so many public-sector bureaucracies, it is shielded from the ultimate customer—other pressure groups move in to fill the vacuum. In some cases this role may be played by the experts, in others, by the trade unions. In many European countries, trade unions have taken advantage of a power vacuum in leaderless public bureaucracies to become the most potent power centers.

In contrast, in successfully run knowledge organizations the leaders are deeply committed people. They love their work, they love to lead, they love their profession, and they love the people they lead. Their emotional commitment rubs off on their followers, whose greatest wish is often to share the leaders' enthusiasm.

So what does it take to run a knowledge organization successfully? It takes recruiting, managing, developing, and motivating the professionals. These are the subjects of the next chapter.

Summary

- There are four major players in the knowledge company: the professional, the manager, the support staff, and the leader.
- The most highly skilled professionals—the experts—are the genuine income generators.
- Experts are characterized by a dedication to their jobs and their professions, a love of solving problems, and a dislike of routine.
- Managers are in many ways the opposite of professionals. They are capable of managing and organizing, have learned to work through other people, and enjoy doing so.
- The support staff assists both the professionals and the managers. They have no special qualifications of their own to give them status in a knowledge organization.
- Leaders are the people whom others want to follow. They are informally "appointed" by their followers. Leadership involves two tasks: deciding where the organization should go and persuading others to follow. The most successful leaders of knowledge organizations are usually former experts, but they are rarely the most outstanding experts.

Advice to Managers

- The experts are the most valuable employees in the organization because they are able to create uniquely new knowledge. The task of the leader is to find the most profitable arena for them to play in.
- The professionals in knowledge organizations are revenue creators; attention should be focused on the revenues they generate, not on the costs they cause. The task of management is to provide professionals with conditions in which they can be creative for the benefit of customers and yet not let the organization become dependent on them.

▪ The managers in a knowledge organization are few and often in conflict with the experts. The task of the leader is to motivate them.

▪ The support staff is often a forgotten lot. The task of the leader is to support them.

6

Keys to Developing and Utilizing Professional Competence

In order to manage competence, there must be an understanding of how employees, and particularly professionals, should be recruited, developed, motivated, and rewarded. The purpose of this book is not to discuss these functions in detail but rather to present some of the strategic issues raised by a knowledge perspective on these topics.

▪ The Objective: To Decrease Dependence on Experts

Most heads of knowledge companies can identify a few key people whom they feel are crucial to the company's survival—the skilled and experienced people who solve the most intricate problems, bring in the biggest fees, and have the widest network of contacts outside the organization. Most of these key people are very skilled professionals. In this book, I call them *the experts*. The company's whole business can often be traced back to the experts. In smaller organizations an expert may have the greatest professional skill and experience and therefore often also be the undisputed managing director, entrepreneur, marketing manager, and personnel manager all in one. It is the professional competence of such key people and their ability to generate revenue that determine whether a knowledge company prospers. And they may even be considered a free resource—because compared to the income they generate they cost nothing.

The dependency is most evident in consulting firms because the relationship between client and consultant is often closer than that between consultant and consulting firm. Consultants spend most of their time with clients and build close working relationships with them. Moreover, consultants receive more praise—which is the spice

---

65

of life for these creative people—from their clients than from their own companies, often for the simple reason that the latter have but a vague idea of what they have been doing.

Reducing the firm's dependence on its key people is one of the chief executive's main tasks. The degree of dependence obviously varies with the type of business. The link between the business and the key people can never be entirely eliminated in knowledge companies because the work itself is a creative process in which individuals are deeply involved. Still, there is considerable scope for reducing dependency in most service companies. A personnel strategy that encompasses recruitment, management, and development can help achieve this objective.

▪ Recruiting in a Competitive Personnel Market

Recruiting new employees is management's most important investment decision and perhaps its most important strategic tool. A knowledge company's recruitment of new staff can be likened to an industrial company's investment in new machinery. By strategic recruitment, management can both modify the company's business idea and increase or reduce its competence and other intangible assets.

The recruitment issue is complicated by the fact that capable new recruits are hard to find. This is a universal problem, not one peculiar to peak economic cycles. Even during the slump of the early 1990s, many companies complained of the shortage of qualified personnel. Many acquisitions of knowledge companies are actually made to secure the people working in those companies and thus are a form of recruitment.

Because experts and professionals with a potential to become experts are in short supply, they choose their places of work with great care. To compete for this pool of talent, wise knowledge organizations compete for them with other knowledge organizations in the same way that they compete for customers: indeed, they treat professionals more like customers than employees. Consequently, knowledge organizations compete in two markets: the market for customers and the market for personnel. Knowledge organization managers need a strategy for personnel markets, just as much as they need one for customer markets. (I prefer the term *personnel market* to *labor market* because it is competence—not labor—that a knowledge organization seeks.)

Managers need a clear idea of the kind of people they want to recruit and they must be ready to compete for them with other companies. Therefore, they must have a plan for making their company as attractive as possible to the people it needs. They need a personnel strategy that, of course, must also be consistent with the customer strategy.

When you have a knowledge perspective, the key selection criteria when interviewing potential recruits are the candidates' knowledge or qualifications and their ability to enhance their own knowledge and that of the firm's other employees. A salary buys access to an individual's time and potential to enhance the firm's ability to increase the yield from all its knowledge. Thus, employees' salaries are less important than the knowledge they contribute, the revenues they generate, and the customers they bring to the organization. It thus makes sense to see an employee as a generator of revenue rather than as a cost.

ꞏꞏ Managing Professionals

As discussed in Chapter 5, the task of the leader is to foster the conditions under which professionals can be most creative. There are several ways to create such conditions.

SECURITY AS A MANAGERIAL TOOL

Professionals work hard and are often plagued by anxiety. They have to turn in first-rate creative performances year after year. They often lack employment security, they find it hard to develop well-rounded personalities, they expose themselves to public criticism, they compete fiercely with one another, they work in constantly changing organizations, and their worth is judged only by what they produce.

When there's a lot of anxiety in the air, security becomes an important tool of leadership. People feel secure if they have confidence in their ability to cope with what lies ahead. Security is thus both the antithesis of and the antidote for anxiety.

Artistic leaders can, deliberately or unwittingly, foster or destroy this sense of security among their team. Swedish film director Ingmar Bergman has always been acutely aware of how vulnerable actors are in their lonely encounters with their audiences. Bergman's method is to imbue them with such confidence in their technical performance that they do not have to think about how they move on stage. Others, like the now–deceased German conductor Herbert von

Karajan, deliberately cultivate a state of insecurity in order to maintain high levels of anxiety among their creative people. Both methods seem to foster creativity, but the latter is not recommended.

VERTICAL DIVISION OF LABOR

As already stated, professionals loathe routine tasks and often succeed in persuading management to introduce vertical specialization: the research lab hires test-tube shakers, the consulting firm recruits number crunchers. However, management can avoid this situation by simply abolishing all assistants, replacing them with professionals, formulating the business mission in such a way as to minimize the number of routine tasks, and then requiring the professionals to perform the routine tasks that remain.

Yet another way around this problem is to use the system that evolved in the traditional craft trades and assign the work according to age—employ young people with potential as the journeymen who undergo training on low-status, routine jobs. This is common practice in the accounting and legal professions, as well as in the larger management consulting firms.

INTANGIBLE REWARDS FOR MOTIVATION

As a part of their marketing strategy, many knowledge companies identify and deliberately exploit the chemistry between their key people and their customers because the better the relationships, the easier it is to win new assignments. This makes such people so valuable that their value is very hard to price, raising in turn the delicate issue of rewards. Fortunately, at least in my experience, professionals are generally not motivated by money. Some readers might argue against this assertion; there are certainly exceptions in some industries and some geographic areas. Still, professionals, and experts in particular, are best motivated by intangible rewards, such as peer recognition, learning opportunities, opportunities for more independence, and so on. Other ideas for motivation can be gleaned from Chapter 5 (particularly the section "A Summary of Characteristics"). Furthermore, when professionals do seem to be motivated by money, like some in the finance industry or Silicon Valley, it should be recognized that money is usually a substitute for something more intangible, like prestige or independence.

Regarding monetary rewards, how much should a key person be paid? I believe the best way to answer this question is to think in terms of value added and to pay key people a reasonable proportion of the value they create. In any event, they should not be paid a fixed salary. Ways to calculate value added are discussed in Chapter 12.

▪ Developing Professionals

Jesus' disciples called Him "Master." Rising to master of a trade is a dream of achievement that is probably as old as human history. The earliest descriptions of the creative career can be found in the annals of the medieval guilds, for in those days it was the craftsmen, and particularly the smiths, who earned their living from knowledge. Although the ranks of master and journeyman are no longer formally recognized, their equivalents survive in modern professions, particularly those in which special skills must be cultivated, such as music. Thus, a student at a conservatory may be considered an apprentice and a graduate from a conservatory a journeyman. Securing a place with a famous orchestra is the next step in a musical career. The few musicians who develop their skills to the utmost and go on to be soloists and virtuosos will eventually hold so-called master classes for their young prodigies.

Developing into an expert is the natural and preferred career path for a professional. Few want to be executives with responsibility for managing others, as a head consultant does. The reason why so many professionals nevertheless welcome promotion to executive rank is that they regard it as a recognition of their worth.

The leader and the soloists in an orchestra are musicians first and foremost. But as the institution of the master class implies, virtuosity carries with it a responsibility for artistic development of others. The natural career path for an expert culminates, by virtue of his or her skill and experience, in the role of teacher and mentor. In an English accounting firm, for example, the chartered accountants wear two hats: executive and teacher of junior colleagues. Similarly, experienced barristers of the English bar have pupils: newly qualified lawyers to whom they impart their wisdom and skill.

WHEN PROFESSIONALS PLATEAU

But the careers of most professionals do not develop in such a neat, orderly way. Many people and much knowledge go to waste as a result of the stress and mismanagement to which the professional is subjected. Creative people, who constantly stretch themselves to the limits of their ability, can be found in most walks of life. Like the mythical Damocles, they live in constant greatness and constant danger. Their lives, like the lives of great artists and virtuosos of all kinds, can be tragically short. Their light shines brightly for a while and is then extinguished. If goals are defined as narrowly and in such concrete terms as those of athletes, for example, the only road left open to those who have reached the top is downhill.

The research world is a battleground for kudos. For example, scientists can never be sure how their work will be judged by other scientists. Recognition is unreliable and arbitrary. What is hailed as a triumph by one group may be viciously attacked by another. The researcher usually stands alone, without allies. No holds are barred in the struggle to secure resources for one's own projects. The struggle is bitter because the contestants are individuals, not institutions, as in the corporate world. Psychosis and drug abuse are common among artists and other public performers, but even more workaday creative professions, such as journalism, wear their practitioners down. A survey by the Swedish Central Bureau of Statistics showed that journalists are likely to die younger than those other in occupations. The survey began with a total of 7,780 professionally active Swedish journalists alive in 1970 and found that within ten years 514 of them had died before the age of sixty-five, for a mortality rate 20 percent higher than the average. The most common cause of death was cancer, but the death rate among journalists from cirrhosis of the liver (usually caused by excessive drinking) was three times the average for other occupational categories. Almost all consultants and creative people go through one or more crises during their careers. They come at intervals of five to ten years and can take any form. They afflict consultants, advertising people, architects, stockbrokers, physicians, and senior civil servants.

When matters have progressed too far, it is too late to do anything about the problem. The person may resign and start over in a new firm, taking customers and colleagues with him or her. The remarkable thing is that the new company is often an instant success. Everyone works hard, assignments pour in, and enthusiasm is sky high—until the next creative crisis.

Various psychological models have been constructed to explain this phenomenon. One common view is that people go through a biological life cycle. The phenomenon is not so noticeable in "ordinary" companies except at the top management level. But the management of a knowledge company must live with the varying life cycles of its creative people and plan the whole organization accordingly.

People generally want to feel that they are building up their skills. They generally want to gain experience by working on challenging projects with other skilled professionals. The young new employee is an apprentice who probably costs more in supervision, training, and assistance than he or she earns for the company. However, these young people do not demand much in the way of encouragement because the prospect of a rapid accumulation of skills provides all the motivation they need.

The ability of professional people to create value increases rapidly as they gain experience but so do their costs, in the form of salaries, secretaries, fringe benefits, and so on. A rapid gain in experience provides motivation in itself, but creative work is very demanding. Eventually, even the best professional will reach a creative plateau.

Management has three options for helping its professionals deal with such a plateau:

1. *Do nothing.* This action creates an overpaid, underperforming professional.
2. *Fire the person.* This is the cost-cutting option. It is quick and simple. It costs severance pay and destroys the relationship but saves future losses.
3. *Find alternative employment for the person who has reached a plateau.* To take this action, management must see the person through the knowledge perspective.

People can create revenues with their competence in various ways: as mentor, teacher, salesperson, ambassador. As mentioned earlier, this is the natural culmination of the professional's career path. Yet the heads of most companies choose the first or second option as a solution to the plateau problem and rarely choose the third.

There is another common situation. The professional recognizes that he or she is approaching a plateau and blames it on the leadership of the company. This often leads to a personal crisis; in extreme cases, it may lead to alcoholism or even suicide. If a company's reputation has faded, if it has not allowed its people to develop their capabilities, or if it has become an organization in which employees feel alienated, the mobile key people will be susceptible to offers from rival firms or will sign up with headhunters.

A firm's employees' abilities are assets that, although not owned by the company, can add luster to its reputation if properly exploited. Clients are aware of the development of the reputations of outstanding employees, so one way to boost a company's reputation is to hire "high flyers," people who are visible and can solve problems more creatively than customers expect.

The life cycles and crises of key persons come as no surprise to successful knowledge companies because they have already planned their organization to deal with these contingencies. They know the kinds of professionals they have and the types of life cycles they are following.

THE PROFESSIONAL'S THREE LIFE CYCLES

At least three life–cycle types can be distinguished: *the superstar, the statesman,* and *the normal professional.* The three are illustrated in Figure 10.

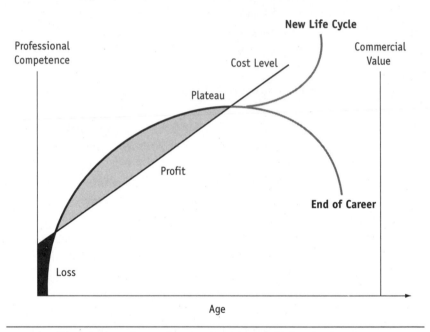

Figure 10. A "normal" professional can go through several life cycles during a career.

The superstar's life cycle is up like a rocket, then down like a stone. It is characterized by a restless, almost explosive creativity that is often coupled with poor judgment. Superstars can accomplish magnificent feats, but their spectacular flops can make even the most hard–bitten executives tear their hair out in desperation. Executives are usually thankful that there are not too many superstars in the firm. Indeed, two is often too many.

The statesman's life cycle is quite different. Such professionals get steadily better as the years go by and are good at establishing personal relations. The archetypes are such politicians as Henry Kissinger, Margaret Thatcher, or Jimmy Carter or business leaders like Marvin Bower of McKinsey and the late David Packard of Hewlett-Packard. Today these people no longer turn in the most outstanding professional performance, but they are wise and can be relied on to generate a growing amount of revenue because of their extensive networks. There are not many statesmen around either, and this is also a blessing because they are usually self-centered and seldom tolerate rivals.

The path of the so-called normal professional lies somewhere between these two extremes, but it is apt to tilt one way or the other.

Real career curves are not, of course, as smooth as those shown in Figure 10. Rather, they are likely to resemble a series of small staircases piled one on top of the other, representing a recurring succession of cycles. Physicians, consultants, and art directors are usually at the peak of their profitability to an organization just before or at the top of their curve or staircase; thus, they are liable to take the first downward step just when the big assignment comes in and they are at their most indispensable.

Is this a scary thought? Not unless you think that all careers must follow a predetermined pattern. It is at this peak point that many managers go wrong because, in a business world still conditioned by the outlook appropriate to the industrial age, they find it hard to grasp the notion that the career path of a professional need not resemble a constantly ascending staircase, and particularly not one that involves, as the industrial model prescribes, increasing responsibility for managing the work of subordinates.

ꞏ¹ A Career Development Strategy: Age Distribution

In periods of crisis, organizations often make the mistake of imposing recruitment bans, thus saddling themselves with large groups of competent, older employees and no plans for further development, leaving no advancement opportunities for the young Turks. This situation causes dissatisfaction among the old and young employees alike. It is becoming commonplace in public sectors throughout the Western world as organizations respond in the least painful way to demands for cost cuts.

Such organizations acquire a spare tire around their waists that creeps out a bit wider each year. Because older people are not interested in doing the same things as younger people, there is a major impact on the organization's business idea. The business idea "ages" along with the employees, and this is very dangerous in the long term, adversely affecting profitability.

Such skewed age distributions can occur as the result of good strategic reasons but have negative and unexpected consequences. For example, thanks to rigorous cost controls, a certain European bank has managed to maintain an above-average profitability for many years but has, in the process, created a staffing situation that could cause much grief later on. In 1975, the bank had five employees in the twenty-five to twenty-nine year age bracket for every one aged fifty-five to fifty-nine. Since it persisted with this policy for such a long time and since there has been little change in the total number of employees, the ratio has been reversed in 1996 and the bank is now experiencing a serious shortage of young managers to groom for higher posts. By disregarding the age structure, the bank's management has set the scene for a period of troublesome shifts, when a new generation of managers will have to be schooled and installed.

Maintaining the right age structure is an important issue for the management of any company, but particularly for knowledge companies. I am not advocating age discrimination. However, management must plan recruitment well ahead of time and regard each new hire as an investment in the future, rather than as a cost that reduces profitability. Furthermore, one cannot look to the experts themselves for ideas in this area; this is management's job.

⁌ A Career Development Strategy: Alternative Career Patterns

Leaders with a knowledge perspective can see alternative career patterns for professionals, patterns that often involve new experiences, travel, and changes of work—including changing career tracks. Successful knowledge organizations know their professionals so well that they can plan this kind of career for them.

This is not to say firms should offer lifetime employment to everyone. Some firms deliberately build short life cycles into their strategies. Few tour guides are over age thirty because tour operations in sunshine resorts seek young, extroverted, adventurous, low-paid people who will only stay for a few years. Similarly, cleaning firms run labor-intensive operations with very high rates of personnel turnover by recruiting immigrants. Fast food restaurants do their recruiting primarily among high school students.

Lifetime employment is the exception, even in consultancy firms. Most firms aim to keep new recruits for an average of ten years, or the equivalent of an annual personnel turnover rate of 10 percent. The large management consulting firms and accounting firms often adopt the "up-or-out" principle made famous by McKinsey, thereby maintaining a turnover of around 10 percent.

Many big firms see an advantage in letting consultants come and go. An employment period of five to seven years may be agreed upon at the time of hiring. In this way, management avoids the responsibility for coping with the employee's many crises and yo-yo life cycle. Indeed, if management gets the timing right, it can employ people just when they do their best work and so earn the maximum money with the minimum management effort. Managers of advertising agencies are quite familiar with "creatives," who flit from agency to agency seeking the next creative kick or life cycle.

What can knowledge companies do to resolve such problems among their professionals? The first step is to decide what kind of careers to offer. The younger the professional, the more important this first step is. Short, medium, or lifetime careers are all feasible, as long as management knows what it wants and adapts the company's strategy accordingly. This chosen strategy then becomes part of the knowledge company's personnel strategy.

Unfortunately, many knowledge companies—especially new ones—ruthlessly exploit their best creative talent without any awareness that they are doing so. It is all too easy to overextend people at the top of a life-cycle curve: management works them hard in production and forgets their need for further development. After a very short time—no more than a year or so in extreme cases—the expert collapses. It may not even be a creative crisis; just plain fatigue can cause harsh words to be spoken and irrevocable decisions to be made.

It does not take much creativity to find solutions to avoid such crises. Instead of high salaries that are just taxed away in any case, a better inducement for a professional may be a "further education account," a part-time research job, a writing job, perhaps a course in painting, or some other intangible reward.

,ı' Deloitte-Touche: Solving the Status Problem

Big customers are status symbols for an accountancy firm and becoming a big-name corporate auditor is thus a major career milestone. So young associates compete to work with senior partners in the hope of eventually "going public." The trouble is, auditing the books of a big public company is not particularly exciting. The work consists mainly of checking figures and ploughing through voucher files and computer printouts. It is actually more educating to audit small companies because the problems are more varied and challenging. But given a choice, most young accountants go for status. How can this problem be solved?

Deloitte–Touche Group, the international accountancy firm, has a mixed bag of companies, both public and private, among its clientele. To persuade young accountants to take an interest in the problems of small firms, a special small business unit was established in the United States as a separate profit center. After a while, the small business unit showed that it was producing more added value and more profit than the public practice. The status of the small business auditors was thus enhanced, and as a result of a profit–sharing scheme they were paid at least as much as those working for the major corporations.

Summary
- In managing competence, the knowledge organization is managing primarily its professionals, and in particular its experts.
- Only wise recruitment, management, and development strategies that take into account the characteristics of the knowledge organization's employees can produce success.
- Knowledge organization managers need a strategy for personnel markets just as much as they need a strategy for customer markets.
- Developing into the role of expert is a natural career for professionals; few want to be responsible for managing others.
- Professionals work hard and are often plagued by anxiety. Giving them a sense of security is often an effective management tool.
- Career development for a professional follows a life–cycle pattern. For professionals to avoid plateaus, knowledge company management should maintain the right age mix.

Advice to Managers
- Managers need to identify the experts, get to know them personally, and create roles and tasks to their satisfaction.
- The values of the experts tend to dominate a knowledge organization. To lead the organization, managers must learn to see those values.

- The best professionals should not be allowed to work all of the time with clients. They must be urged to develop their competence in other areas and to take part in R&D projects. Unguided, they tend to narrow their focus.
- Managers need to scout their organization for professionals who might develop into mentors, teachers, and leaders.
- The use of low-qualified assistants is a policy that should be avoided. They create an inefficient vertical division of labor. It is better to hire more professionals or let the junior professionals do the assistant work in apprenticeships.
- Recruitment is the equivalent of an investment decision and should be treated as such—as a top management priority.
- Mainly highly educated people should be recruited because they have been trained in the most valuable activity of this era: knowledge conversion.
- Competence is best transferred by tradition—by doing. Experienced blue-collar workers and craftsmen possess a tacit knowledge that is possible to transfer only by tradition. Professionals should be seen as masters and teachers, not as lecturers.
- Job rotation should become the policy even if it was tried previously and subsequently abandoned.
- A company's age structure should be managed so that the spare-tire effect does not occur.
- There is an upper limit on how much a person can produce in added value, but the limit can be pushed further through investments in information technology.

Building Internal Structure to Support Knowledge Transfer

The internal structure is the flow of knowledge within an organization—the patents, concepts, models, and computer and administrative systems that support the professionals who are involved in the knowledge creation process with customers. Because the employees combine with the internal structure to constitute the organization, managing the internal structure means managing the organization.

Organizational management is a vast area, discussion of which is beyond the scope of this book. I will focus on four key sets of internal structures. In this chapter, I will discuss the three that involve operational aspects: the tension between professionals and managers, the production process in knowledge organizations, and methods to manage and improve knowledge conversion without information technology. The fourth will be discussed in Chapter 8.

Managing Tension

Within a knowledge organization, the tension between professionals and their customers and between professionals and managers is a critical internal structure that must be managed.

THE MOMENT OF TENSION

There is something special about performing before an audience. Both conductors and directors acknowledge the importance of the audience; some even claim that the audience participates in the performance by releasing the creativity of the players and that when the magic works, players and audience together can lift a performance to sublime heights. This moment of tension is what actors live for, and the same feeling is experienced by a consultant when making an important pitch to a customer.

The moment of tension plays a vital role in creative problem solving. The results of creativity are sporadic and unpredictable, so leaders who want their organizations to be creative must be prepared to put up with unpredictable lurches, first this way and then that, in moods and emotions. And because flops and failure are inevitable, they must be seen as educational experiences by leaders of creative people. A friend once said to me, after one of my less successful efforts, "Don't look on it as a failure. You can always cite it as a cautionary tale."

Managers must understand this process and how it affects their professionals' behavior and performance.

TENSION BETWEEN PROFESSIONALS AND MANAGERS

As discussed in Chapters 4 and 5, professionals are linked to a professional tradition with a value system that exists outside their organization. These professional values tend to compete with those of the managers, who are there to take care of the organization. This creates a tension. Using these tensions as fuel for moving an organization forward is one of the keys to successful leadership of knowledge organizations.

To use this tension, management must understand that its power comes primarily from the control of its representatives—the managers and leaders—over the corporate purse strings. In contrast, the power of the professionals derives from their own skills and, when they work in the private sector, from their ability to earn revenue for their companies.

The struggle between creative and administrative forces goes on in all organizations that are dependent on professionals. Theaters and orchestras are two extreme examples; other examples range from film and television companies to churches, monasteries, and circuses. Although the differences between managers and professionals can easily explode into literally disastrous conflict, skillful leaders can channel these tensions into controlled explosions of creative energy. To do this, managers can learn from enterprises such as theaters, orchestras, and newspapers, which employ creative people and have developed various techniques to channel the tensions. One such technique is *tandem leadership*.

TANDEM LEADERSHIP

In tandem leadership, a director, conductor, or editor is appointed to run the artistic side of a business, while a producer, manager, or publisher takes charge of the administrative staff. Tandem leadership, with one leader running the professionals and the other running the business, would not have evolved in so many otherwise unrelated businesses if it did not work. Both professionals and administrators are necessary to an organization. If an organization consists entirely of professionals, the result is total chaos; nothing is produced. But with only administrators, as in a battery, there is no creative spark. The combination of the creative genius of Charles Saatchi and the business acumen of his younger brother Maurice propelled their advertising agency to a position of short-lived world leadership. When the withdrawal of Charles Saatchi destroyed the intimacy of the link between the creative and business leaderships, it was only a matter of time before the business fell apart. Hans Mellström and Thord Wilkne, the founders of WM-data, the only remaining independent major computer consultancy firm in Sweden, are a similar tandem leadership couple.

If, as many observers believe, all organizations are becoming more like knowledge organizations, then those who wish to enhance the creativity of their companies should look closely at the tandem leadership systems that evolved in publishing and the performing arts, which have much more experience in managing the creative prima donnas.

THE RESULTS OF UNMANAGED TENSION

Unmanaged tension can be detrimental in several ways. Unless given alternatives, professionals and managers tend to develop their competence along different paths. A career path that alternates between managerial and professional responsibilities, as practiced in some American companies (such as IBM, which pioneered this process) and most Japanese companies, serves the purpose of giving both groups a common language for knowledge creation. Because managers and professionals generally have different responsibilities in organizations, it is all too easy to underscore the negative tension. For instance, applying different remuneration systems and assigning different levels of status are dangerous practices. The differences between the two groups are also emphasized by the curriculum of business schools that still favors management of manufacturing companies. In contrast, little organizational knowledge has been accumulated on how to manage knowledge organizations and professionals.

Because the tension is often not managed but merely suppressed or misunderstood, managers and professionals often find themselves involved in a power play. Some industries, like the media industry, have dug particularly deep trenches; the power play between the editors and the managers can be quite heated. When a firm's leaders are unable to understand or control its dynamics, the organization becomes, in effect, leaderless, and it will automatically align itself with the forces acting on it and within it. When a knowledge organization is left to find its own orientation in this way, it invariably chooses to align itself with professional values; in other words, the experts take over.

The Barings, Daiwa, and Sumitomo disasters illustrate what can happen when managers relinquish control to experts, but it is quite wrong to assume, as most commentators on the Barings debacle insisted, that the way to manage these risks is to exert more managerial control over the professionals. This will invariably choke their creativity. The problem with Barings was not lack of *management control* but rather lack of *leadership*. The men at the top did not understand the derivatives markets well enough, and they did not understand that the money they earned was a result of how they managed their intangible assets. They were entirely focused on the tangible money flows, they based the remuneration system entirely on commissions earned, and they did not know their staff very well personally. They had not created their own corporate knowledge about derivatives but relied on the competence of a few individuals instead. In short, Barings top managers were not knowledge-focused.

ꜚ Production in Knowledge Organizations

Production in knowledge organizations includes three structures: *knowledge conversion, the chemistry between professionals and customers,* and *the understanding that knowledge organizations have operating leverage.*

KNOWLEDGE CONVERSION

In knowledge organizations, tacit knowledge is converted into an explicit form (information) in two ways: either concepts and models are combined into new forms or knowledge is externalized. For example, a computer programmer who is making an order entry system combines explicit rules of procedure into algorithms that can be handled by a computer. Accountants combine several sources of information into reports. Architects externalize their mental models of three-dimensional buildings into two-dimensional drawings. Management consultants externalize their interpretation of a company's organization or strategy into oral or written recommendations.

The production process in manufacturing firms can be seen as knowledge conversion too—in R&D, computing, and accounting, for example. Marketers are combining and externalizing when they describe products in brochures and advertisements, and production planning engineers externalize their tacit knowledge of the production process in drawings and diagrams.

GATHERING, REDUCING, AND PRESENTING

Although there are many feedback loops in knowledge conversion, a general structure for producing knowledge can often be discerned. Let's take journalism, for example. A journalist first gathers (combines and internalizes) explicit knowledge, mostly in the form of information, by reading and interviewing. The information already exists in the chaos of reality; it is just a matter of finding it, interpreting it, and reducing the chaos so that the information "fits" and can be presented on a small, two-dimensional piece of paper, or in a few minutes of radio or television broadcast time. The journalistic contribution to the value creation process is the reduction of the chaos of information by using the tricks of the trade. By developing an angle, for example, the journalist can focus in on one small area of reality. Readers may not like the angle chosen, but some angle is essential because an article is not readable unless it is focused. Most information-processing work has the same gathering, reducing, and presenting structure.

The time occupied by each stage, however, varies with the nature of the process. Journalists and researchers spend a lot of time on the initial stage; in advertising it is the last stage that takes the most time. The stage that creates the most value is usually reduction, even though it may not take very long. The ability to reduce a complex reality to a few attention-getting words, metaphors, graphics, or pictures is generally recognized to be the prime hallmark of journalistic talent.

Every profession develops its own methods. Accountants have collectively developed a highly structured presentation format—the balance sheet—whereas architects structure information as lines and pictures. Journalists create copy by combining information from various sources, and because publishers want the result to be read by as many people as possible, the editor devotes considerable resources—space and specialist skills—to presenting it.

Management consultants, too, devote considerable resources to presentation, but in their case it is the person of the consultant, rather than his or her report, that has to be persuasive.

THE FLAWS IN THE PRODUCTION PROCESS

In their efforts to minimize the impact of their own tacit knowledge, research scientists often ignore the presentation stage altogether. The taken-for-grantedness of tacit knowledge is a large problem not only for scientists but for all knowledge workers. Their own skills are both their greatest assets and their greatest liabilities. The expert's tacit knowledge is always there and always colors the end result.

Psychologists tend to view the world in psychological terms, accountants reduce everything to problems in economics, journalists think the world can be saved by the articles they write, and software artists see reality as reducible to computer programs. The copy written by journalists and researchers contains much less information than they collect and reveals only a fragment of the complex reality they are trying to describe. Thus, we always find "mistakes" in newspaper articles when we know some of the background. Sometimes they are real mistakes, but more often they are the consequence of the simplifications needed to fit complete sets of knowledge into highly reduced publishing formats. Journalists are often criticized for distorting reality. The tabloids, in particular, draw highly simplified pictures of reality. But this usually has more to do with the desire to boost circulation than with incompetent reporting. Believe it or not, journalists have codes and professional ethics designed to prevent their tacit knowledge from distorting reality.

Administrators, consultants, and investigators have the same problem. Their reports, however objectively written, are no less slanted than a journalist's articles—the distortion is just harder to detect. Researchers are very conscious of the problem and try to cover all its manifestations in their writing. This is why doctoral dissertations are usually so dull!

In our information-intensive society, more and more of us are engaged in converting information into knowledge and knowledge into information. This explicit knowledge product usually takes the form of information. In this process of gathering, reducing, and presenting, oversimplication and self–interest color the result and become part of the structure.

MATCHING PROFESSIONALS WITH CUSTOMERS: A MATTER OF CHEMISTRY

Customization became a key business theme in the 1980s. It was expressed in slogans like "The customer is king" and "We try harder." In their constant efforts to attract customers, companies promise to do everything in their power, and often much more besides, to accommodate them. But for firms whose business logic is heavily dependent on people, the problem with the customer supremacy idea is that providing service involves close personal contact and *the moment of truth*.

THE MOMENT OF TRUTH

In the early 1980s, Swedish management consultant Richard Normann used the term *moment of truth* to describe the vital meeting between service supplier and customer. The term became widely known after it was adopted by Scandinavian Airlines System (SAS). The moment–of–truth metaphor is very appropriate for large service systems. The staff of a bank, hotel, or restaurant or the cabin crew of an aircraft have brief encounters with many customers each day, and so the main management challenge is to maintain the quality of service and motivation of the staff despite the high volume and repetitive work.

The best–known solution is the "McDonald's method," in which all employees are required to conform to a minutely detailed code of behavior. Sometimes the codes or checklists are presented as derivatives of high–level abstractions called visions or mission statements. But the McDonald's method is not much help when the work of a company consists of joint problem solving with customers in long–term projects. For one thing, the interaction with the customer is far more intense, and for another, the work calls for creativity because the end result can never be known at the outset. It's a process of discovering truth that is controlled not only by the knowledge and qualifications of those involved but also by their ability to find creative solutions to problems in a prolonged collaboration.

The customer plays a vital role, not simply as a source of information and specialized knowledge but also as a catalyst for creativity. The encounter with the customer creates the stimulation or energy that is needed to trigger creativity. The knowledge creation takes place in a process of energy between staff and customers. Thus, those responsible for assigning people to projects must take into account the way employees communicate and how well they are likely to get along with the other project members, including colleagues and customer representatives. People are individuals, each with a distinctive personality. They prefer working with people they can get along well with.

The quest for the secret of personal compatibility is as old as humanity. Most adults have their own ideas about the kind of people they get along with based on their experience, and there are also numerous psychological methods for determining the optimal composition of management groups or teams. I have no favorite method. I simply note the obvious fact that when assembling teams, it is essential to take personal chemistry into account—personal chemistry is an essential internal structure.

Good personal chemistry is not a matter of similarity—people with very different personalities have been shown to find highly creative solutions to problems—but of compatibility. By creating moments that generate energy, personality differences can be important triggers of creativity. The personal chemistry of a group is not a measure of how harmonious it is but of how well its members communicate with one another.

Personal chemistry at work has become quite a hot topic in recent years in the form of team building and team learning, but it has yet to receive the attention it deserves. Most of us still make the mistake of assuming that most people act rationally in their respective roles. Teamwork and personal chemistry are vital in organizations where customers have a decisive influence on outcomes because they too are individuals who get along better with some people than with others. An ability to match experts with customers is an invaluable art for a knowledge organization for two further reasons: first, personal chemistry determines a group's flexibility and how creatively it seeks solutions to unexpected problems; second, it also plays a major role in determining how customers perceive project outcomes. It follows, therefore, that a crucial strategic issue for all knowledge–oriented companies is the selection of suitable customers.

THE VIRTUOUS OR VICIOUS CIRCLE

The problem of matching one's own people to customers is most critical in knowledge organizations, where it involves a number of dilemmas. Depending on how well management resolves them, the firm may enter either a *virtuous* or a *vicious circle.*

The virtuous circle makes it easier to attract both customers and key people, and thus easier to form teams that function smoothly and find good solutions to customer problems, which enhance the company's reputation. But, unfortunately, it is just as easy to enter into a vicious circle, in which management experiences increasing difficulty in attracting customers and qualified people. Personal chemistry between teams and customers becomes progressively harder to manage, customers grow more and more dissatisfied, the firm's reputation suffers, and it becomes harder still to attract customers and employees.

A knowledge organization is constantly balanced between these dynamic circles, or *attractors* as chaos theorists call them, and is seldom in a state of equilibrium. It is either moving rapidly upward or equally rapidly downward. Typical trigger points between the circles are the gain or loss of a key customer or the resignation or recruitment of a key employee. These events should be seen by managers as indicators of staff–customer chemistry.

OPERATING LEVERAGE IN KNOWLEDGE ORGANIZATIONS

Capacity usage generally determines the short–term profitability of all firms because a small change in the extent to which capacity is used has a disproportionate impact on the bottom line. For example, Dutch airline KLM filled 68 percent of its seats in 1992 and lost $300 million. Two years later it achieved 73 percent occupancy and made a profit of over $200 million. The same operating leverage applies in media businesses; an unsold minute of advertising time or an unsold page of space can never be recovered. That is why media companies are so sensitive to market swings.

Capacity usage is also the key to profitability in companies that have mainly intangible assets. In a knowledge organization, the staff is such an important production factor that capacity is effectively fixed in the short term. Moreover, solutions to problems cannot be put on the shelf and sold later. Some 75 percent of a knowledge organization's costs are remuneration, so it is obvious that capacity usage is of crucial importance in controlling its short–term profitability. For instance, if the software consulting company WM–data decreases or increases the number of hours billed during a week by 2.5 percent, this translates into a 20 percent change in operating profit. If the capacity utilization drops by more than 10 percent, WM–data operates in the red.

Even though using some excess capacity for internal R&D projects or training puts a strain on cash flow and such investments do not pay off until later, they are ways of maintaining a high usage factor. And in a knowledge organization, operating leverage exists, and so capacity utilization matters.

❧ Structures to Improve Knowledge Transfer

Techniques for expressing and transferring knowledge in the form of information are abundant. Many systems for information sharing are now available. In their standard form they in-source an on-line system for OCR reading, storage and retrieval of vital documents, an e-mail system, conferencing, and word processing. Information technology systems that store documents or texts are useful as a kind of sophisticated archive system and a support in the knowledge conversion mode combination. But I want to focus on managing the three noncomputerized structures for transferring tacit knowledge,[1] all of which were introduced in Chapter 4: *externalization, socialization,* and *internalization.*

EXPRESSING KNOWLEDGE EXTERNALLY

People usually express knowledge externally in the form of information because information is easy to produce with information technology. Many managers tend to believe that a word written is a word understood. They forget that the receiver of information, not the giver, gives it meaning. (See Chapter 4 for more on this.) In fact, information is so inefficient in transferring tacit knowledge that managers relying on memos or videos get little done. When a complex message is to be communicated or an organizational change implemented, information is more or less useless. As Barry Harrington, developer of the knowledge-sharing system for the management consulting firm Bain, asserts, "For all the technological wizardry contained in complex IT-systems, nothing can replace good old-fashioned talk."[2]

Talk is slightly better than written information, better still is showing what you mean, and best is letting people create the knowledge themselves. This is where socialization and internalization come into play.

SOCIALIZATION USING THE OPEN-OFFICE SPACE

The editorial offices of newspapers are usually large, open-plan spaces, abuzz with noise, full of computers, and littered with pieces of paper and empty boxes. The journalists sit in their cubbyholes or work areas in front of desks that are invariably invisible under mountains of paper. Instead of being overtly creative, they spend most of their time in the office either on the phone or chatting with each other. The cool, calm atmosphere one associates with intellectual endeavor is conspicuous by its absence.

Newspaper offices are like this because editors know that open-plan space facilitates rapid information and knowledge transfer. Just by being present, you can absorb all you need to know to function as a journalist. You do not have to spend time sitting in on briefings or writing and reading reports. Tacit knowledge is created without deliberation or reporting systems. Most person–to–person communication is tacit—out of the corner of the eye—and unconscious. Everyone can see the stars preening themselves and the less successful professionals keeping low profiles. This teaches codes of behavior and skills. In an open–plan area, it soon becomes obvious who the leaders are and it is hard to hold a position of authority without having a talent for it.

Moreover, the pecking order is constantly reconfiguring itself as the situation changes, people leave and enter the space, and the changing topic of conversation shifts the spotlight of acknowledged authority from one expert to another. A journalist who is closeted in a room or starts working from home thus quickly loses competence. Some journalists prefer to sit in isolation because they cannot concentrate on their writing in a boisterous atmosphere, but they are also the ones who complain most often about being cut off from the flow of information and who feel left out of things. People need to communicate face to face, which is the reason why I do not believe that distance working will be the predominant pattern of the future.

The open space is probably the most efficient method of face-to-face communication so far devised. Computer experts would probably describe it as a constantly reconfigured real–time, broadband information channel. This is the way that much human knowledge is passed from generation to generation in the home or on the job. Thus, the editorial room is the externalization of a long tradition of editors' management of knowledge. It is very effective because all knowledge conversion modes are supported.

The open–space office is used for this purpose in many companies; Hewlett-Packard, for instance, has made it compulsory in all its subsidiaries.

SOCIALIZATION USING PIGGYBACKING AND TEAMS

Piggybacking is another structure for creating an arena where senior professionals may show their skills for juniors to imitate. For example, at *Affärsvärlden,* the Swedish magazine for which I worked in the 1980s, we used the method for transferring some of the tricks of the trade to junior writers; a senior journalist was on duty and had to write the article, but a junior writer accompanied the senior writer to interviews and press conferences and assisted in the writing.

The piggybacking method has several advantages in journalism: the tacit techniques of the profession are learned on the job, the network improves fast for the new staff, and the assignment can be discussed among more well-informed people. However, the method is not common in the media industry. It often came as a surprise to the interviewees that *Affärsvärlden* arrived with two or three reporters rather than just one, as was normal for the dailies and other journals. The trend in the media industry is, on the contrary, to build up images of individual journalists, which encourages competition and reduces willingness to share knowledge.

Piggybacking is used frequently in many professions. The larger accounting firms and management consulting firms staff their teams with at least one very junior member who has the double task of doing the dirty work and observing and learning.

Another arena for piggybacking is the project team; if a project needs three skilled people to accomplish the task, a fourth junior professional is added. Piggybacking is used by most large consulting firms for this purpose. We used it at *Affärsvärlden;* larger articles were run as projects, staffed both to enhance the knowledge creation and to help juniors gain knowledge.

INTERNALIZATION USING SIMULATION

Practical knowledge is best transferred when using our whole bodies. That is why games, simulations, and role playing are so effective in transferring knowledge. They pass it on in ways that emulate tradition.

Educational consultant Klas Mellander has helped me to externalize my tacit managerial knowledge into a simulation model that we call Tango 3. It is a tool for transferring knowledge, a tool for teaching managers how to manage intangible assets—how to create a business from knowledge.

In a Tango simulation, up to thirty participants sit in groups of four or five at separate tables, each with an identical game board in front of them. For two days—during which players enact up to seven years of a simulated business's life—they act as the management of their own knowledge company that is in competition with the other groups. A facilitator is present to clarify the rules, organize the market, and act as referee. To maximize knowledge transfer, all the teams are in the same room. A successful Tango simulation resembles an arena where participants learn through the natural broadband channel. They usually enjoy the game; this is important, because we know people learn best if they find learning pleasurable. The atmosphere in Tango simulations is often very intense. People learn a lot of things at once, from one another and from the game itself.

But one cannot predict what players will learn any more than one can predict what anyone will learn in any form of adult education. For some, insights into the measuring of intangible assets is the most important lesson; for others, it may be the interaction within groups; for others again it may be the strategy, or the view of the market, that is illuminated. What people learn depends on what they already know, and they learn it from each other in a process, not from a lecturer or a teacher.

The facilitator supports rather than teaches. This may feel awkward to those accustomed to holding the floor, but adults must discover for themselves what is relevant to them personally. A simulation model throws open the arena to the participants and thus changes the nature of the process from teaching to learning.

A TANGO SIMULATION
The following section was written by journalist Awiwa Keller Dagens Nyheter and has been translated from Swedish.

There were fourteen of us here, all managers, playing Tango. We had never met before, and none of us had ever been exposed to this kind of exercise.

We were divided at random into five groups: three groups of two men and one woman, two men in one group, and two women and one man in my group.

FIRST DAY AT SCHOOL
On the table, in front of us, lay a totally incomprehensible game board. We exchanged anxious looks. Was there an accountant in the house? No. Ah well, we reassured each other, it's only a game.

Our first task was to work out which of the intangible assets are owned by the company. We suggested reputation, know-how, image, routines, good personnel policy, synergies, concepts, and so on. We agreed that the main intangible assets consisted of "reputation capital" and "knowledge capital," essential parts of the company's assets.

PERSONAL CHEMISTRY

Then we discussed interpersonal relations, and the decisive part they play in a knowledge company's business. As play proceeded, we soon realized how crucial personal chemistry between the customer's representative and our own people is to the success of a project. An ability to recruit, develop, and keep the right key people turns out to be vital in this kind of company.

What were the central and most important characteristics of the consultants and customers? We felt challenging assignments would enhance our reputation on the market. If we succeed, we also enhance our own competence. With a good reputation, we will be unbeatable on the market. We had barely gotten started, but felt we were on the right track.

At half-time, we were well on the way. We got the customers we wanted, without having to tempt our personnel with bonuses, and decided to take on more challenging assignments. We would have liked to have a little more equity, but we had not expected to be a profit machine in the first few years.

They say that the best way to do good business is to avoid bad business. Now we had to stop "wasting" overqualified talent on old customers. They weren't paying so well any more.

Time for review: had we held the career talks we had promised and promoted people to the right level of competence? Should we seek new customers, or get rid of old ones?

A GOOD MOVE

Our staff were working at 94 percent of capacity, but the revenues were still too small. Taking on new customers, or phasing out old ones, would cost too much. We decided on a slight change of tack—putting more into R&D, and pressing ahead with the customers we had.

It was a good move. After five years in business, we were the winners on the market. It was with some pride that the three of us, none of us economists in real life, acknowledged the plaudits of our peers.

Alas, there were no cash prizes or diplomas, but what we did get out of it was insight and, not least, some lessons. For example, that things can change fast in knowledge companies, and that the business logic depends heavily on how knowledge organizations view their invisible assets.

LEARNING POINTS FROM TANGO SIMULATIONS

A Tango session is a very powerful thing. A one–day session not only changes the perspectives of the participants but also gives them a number of ideas for action. However, a change of perspective can sometimes be seen as dangerous. I first encountered this odd perception in the United Kingdom, when one of the players in a Tango simulation, a high–level manager, said he would never dare expose his staff to the experience because "it would put a lot of ideas in their heads, and they would start questioning what we are doing."

Furthermore, follow–up is essential. A Tango–type simulation should not be planned to be a one–time course but rather to form part of a larger executive development scheme or strategy process. This makes it necessary for the user of a simulation to understand the context and where it fits into the process. The experience should be used as an inspiration for a critical examination of one's own business. A simulation is only as good as the thought and the "aftercare" devoted to it. There is always a danger that the enthusiasm and competitiveness generated by a simulation will reduce the exercise to playing a game and producing a winner. A couple of hours spent after the session coupling the fresh experience with the reality is time well spent.

An obvious shortcoming of this process is that although a good simulation is similar to reality it is not the same as reality. A simulation model is articulated knowledge, a distillation of a model builder's tacit knowledge of what he or she perceives as reality. It is thus tainted by built-in value judgments that may not match other people's ideas of what the world is like. Another drawback is that it may not be easy to assign so many resources to a program or spare so many people at once to take part in a simulation. Although the efficiency of a simulation, in terms of amount learned per unit of time, is high, it takes longer and demands more of the participants than a series of lectures on a traditional manager's day, for example. It should be noted, however, that this criticism reflects an industrial rather than a knowledge perspective of business.

OTHER ARENAS FOR INTERNALIZATION

The arenas for internalization need not be as sophisticated as a business game. For example, in 1993 Matsushita launched a companywide policy to reduce yearly working time to 1,800 hours (Nonaka and Takeuchi 1995). The policy's objective was not to reduce costs but to change the mindset of managers. But many managers were puzzled about how to implement the policy, which was at first communicated as explicit knowledge. Matsushita created a promotion office with the task to facilitate experiments with the policy for one month by working 150 hours. Through this kind of bodily experience, employees got to know what an 1,800-hour year would be like.

Summary

- The flow of information within an organization—between staff and customers and among the staff—is a structure. If managed properly, the competence of the organization increases, and the relations with customers are improved; customer relations, an external asset, are discussed in the next chapter.
- The difference between the professional tradition and the organizational tradition creates a tension that can energize projects. But it can also initiate a power play. If the top managers do not understand the forces, the experts control the organization.
- The tension between professionals and managers can manifest itself in creativity or in a balance of terror. To benefit from this tension, some successful companies employ a dual or "tandem" leadership system.
- Knowledge workers convert knowledge into explicit knowledge, which usually takes the form of information.
- The encounter with the customer creates energy that triggers creativity. Chemistry between customer and professional relays energy to the organization. A crucial strategic issue for all knowledge-oriented companies is the selection of suitable customers.
- Capacity usage determines the short-term profitability of service firms.
- There are three noncomputerized structures for transferring tacit knowledge: socialization via open office space, socialization via piggybacking and teams, and internalization via simulation.

Advice to Managers

- It is best to treat people in general as revenues, not as costs.

- The tension between managers/administrators and experts can be used to release creative energy. If unmanaged, the tension may develop into severe conflict.

- It is a good idea to create tandem couples consisting of an expert and a manager who have a good chemistry between them. Natural tandem couples that emerge should not be broken up.

- The distinction should be made between leadership of the organization and leadership of the experts. These two roles are very different and the qualifications are rarely combined in one person.

- Two career paths with equal status and remuneration patterns should be created, one managerial and one professional. People should be encouraged to move between the two careers. This is the way to create new leaders.

- Experts should be given the same remuneration and information as managers, no matter what their formal rank. The best experts should have a higher remuneration than their bosses.

- The capacity utilization of a company's professionals must be monitored; that's where the profit leverage is.

- Offices should be designed as open spaces in order to utilize the full human ability to absorb knowledge unconsciously.

- It is not advisable to construct a separate administration building for the managers and officers because this will only enlarge the rift between managers and experts.

- High personnel turnover and absenteeism is a warning sign that an organization's intangible assets are rapidly being drained.

Improving Efficiency and Effectiveness through Internal Structure

The effect of size on efficiency and effectiveness—that is, on the internal structures—in a knowledge organization is largely misunderstood. Yet, it has strategic implications as to how the organization chooses to grow. These implications are the topic of the first part of this chapter.

An additional structure will also be covered. This book proposes that it is important to be knowledge-focused, that small is better, that intangible assets have more worth than tangible assets. But in reality most existing organizations are a long way from this ideal. Is it possible to move from today's reality to this ideal, to be both knowledge-focused and industrial, to have large tangible assets and still utilize the intangible assets, to be both small and large? I believe that it is possible; in fact, that is probably the route that large organizations will tend to take. The final section of this chapter explores a way to design an internal structure to accomplish this.

▪ Efficiency

Effectiveness is generally defined as an indicator that relates output to input. *Efficiency* and *productivity* are usually considered to be synonyms and only refer to measurement of input variables. These definitions come from an industrial perspective. But, as was discussed in Chapter 2, knowledge organizations have different characteristics than industrial organizations, and these characteristics invalidate these concepts when they are applied to knowledge organizations.

◂ Big Is Not Better

Since Richard Arkwright invented the factory system at the end of the eighteenth century, the manufacturing industry has sought efficiency through specialization and volume, based on the idea that larger companies can distribute their fixed costs—that is, the costs of administration, machinery, and R&D—over a larger volume and thus achieve higher profitability.

Research by the European Union on small and medium-sized enterprises (SMEs),[1] those with 1 to 499 employees, has shown that whereas SMEs are less efficient than larger enterprises in capital-intensive industries like manufacturing and mining, small knowledge firms (producer services in Figure 11) are more productive than their larger counterparts. Other research corroborates these results. Thus, in the service sector, efficiency seems to diminish with increasing size, especially in areas where capital intensity is low, as in knowledge organizations. (See Figure 11.)

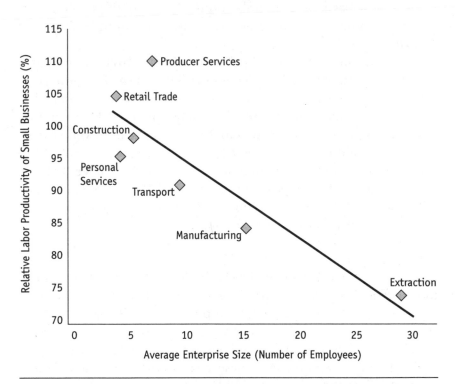

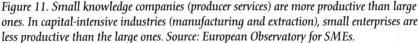

Figure 11. Small knowledge companies (producer services) are more productive than large ones. In capital-intensive industries (manufacturing and extraction), small enterprises are less productive than the large ones. Source: European Observatory for SMEs.

The main reason is that creative people generally dislike work-ing for large organizations, and so they either leave them or perform below their full potential there. This phenomenon is validated by experienced managers in knowledge organizations who often say that fifty employees is the threshold number. At that point the small, tightly knit family—where everyone knows what's going on—is obliged, if it wants to keep growing, to assume a more formal struc-ture and hire professional managers. Swedish software consultant WM–data employs thirty–eight hundred but stipulates that no single unit should comprise more than fifty people.

In other words, unlike industrial organizations, knowledge orga-nizations are not more effective as their size increases. But does knowledge increase efficiency or productivity?

THE ADVANTAGE OF HIGH COMPETENCE

That an organization would be more efficient if its employees were more competent seems a logical conclusion. But it is very hard to prove. Two Swedish business magazines, *Affärsvärlden* (AFV) and *Veckans Affärer* (VA), provide an illuminating test of the proposition.

VA had pursued a traditional organizational track ever since its founding in 1965; that is, it aimed for volume to achieve advantages of scale. AFV, relaunched in 1975, focused on building superior skills among its staff to establish an edge in the quality of its financial analyses. (AFV's knowledge strategy will be discussed further in Chapter 10.)

As shown in Figure 12, VA, not surprisingly, has held a consistent lead in circulation.

The two magazines had been fierce competitors ever since 1975. Although they worked under different editorial concepts, toward the end of the 1980s readers perceived both as on a par in terms of qual-ity.

As shown in Figure 13, AFV was able to achieve a higher profit margin (Sveiby 1994) than VA, even though the latter, being larger, reported a higher total profit.

What made AFV's journalists twice as productive as VA's and how did they keep it up for fifteen years? So great a productivity gap between two such similar businesses over such a long period of time could not be explained by different markets, efforts of individual employees, differences in pay, or economic cycles. There had to be another reason. We found three plausible explanations:

Circulation 1966–1992

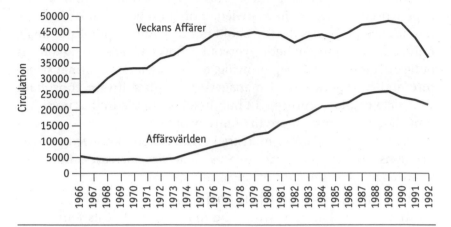

Figure 12. Affärsvärlden *and* Veckans Affärer: *circulation figures.*

1. Some 30 percent of the difference in margin was due to the difference in format. AFV's design was simpler, had fewer illustrations, and thus needed fewer layout artists.
2. About 30 percent of the difference during the first five or so years after 1975 was due to AFV's journalists working between one and two hours a day longer than VA's.
3. The rest of the difference—some 40 percent during the first years and perhaps as much as 70 percent during the last years—

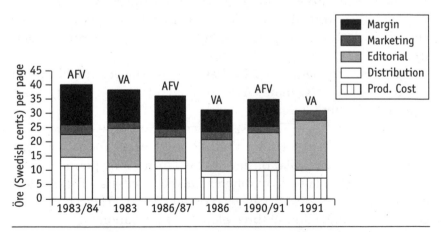

Figure 13. Affärsvärlden *and* Veckans Affärer: *cost comparison.*

remained unexplained unless a third factor was brought in: a difference in competence.

Unlike most of VA's editorial staff, all AFV journalists were academically trained in financial analysis, which increased their ability to analyze problems and process information. As a result, they could work faster, asking fewer but more relevant questions than journalists at the rival magazine. Although conventionally trained journalists had to phone around, using their contacts to find experts who might or might not have the answers, AFV's journalists could do more of their work at their desks. I believe that about half the difference in productivity could be attributed to the difference in educational background.

⁚⁣ Being Effective with a Knowledge Focus

Effectiveness brings revenue into the efficiency equation and, as we have seen, much of this revenue is not measured. The leaders of large knowledge companies may acknowledge that their companies are less efficient than their smaller rivals, but they argue in effectiveness terms and point, for example, to the marketing advantages of size in an industry in which image and reputation are vital.

The largest firms get the most assignments and, even more important, the largest assignments, and therefore they become better known. They are approached more often when interesting projects come up and they find it easier to recruit staff. These were the motives for the wave of accounting firm mergers in the 1987 to 1991 period all over the world. Accountants cite another motive: they say they must follow the customers. If the customers—often major industrial corporations—are expanding globally, accountants must do likewise to retain their customers.

There are some advantages of scale in the knowledge business, especially in relation to research and development, computer systems, and specialist skills. There are also advantages of scale in certain capital-intensive knowledge companies, where financial capital is an important resource, such as fund management and investment banking. But the advantages of scale in knowledge organizations have little to do with production efficiency or (financial) capital utilization. They have more to do with how well intangible assets are used and should be seen more as economies of scope than as economies of scale.

VOLUME GROWTH AND SUCCESS

Volume growth is not necessarily a sign of success. *Organic growth*, as its name implies, is the natural kind of growth that occurs when the business concept is so strong and the level of knowledge so high that the company's knowledge is sought by more and more customers. A company that grows organically thus demonstrates that its business concept is appreciated by the market. In such cases, there need be no hesitation in equating growth with success. But a firm that grows simply by acquiring other companies has confused cause with effect.

The classic problem of organic growth is quality control. New employees, often scattered in offices all over the country—or all over the world—need to be trained and guided by senior professionals and middle management. This increases the complexity of the firm and tends to undermine the professional quality of the work.

The organic growth of knowledge companies is limited by their ability to recruit new potential experts of the right quality and their ability to lead, manage, and control larger and more complex organizations. Since the supply of experts and potential experts is always limited, organizations that grow organically must devote more and more resources to in-house education, on-the-job training, and recruitment of suitable young people. Because of the constraints imposed by complexity and the limited supply of potential experts, it seems hard to sustain a long-term annual growth rate of more than about 10 percent through organic growth alone, even if the market is expanding faster than that.

McKinsey grew by almost 15 percent a year between 1989 and 1994 and the company itself recognizes the quality risk such rapid growth entails. The firm cannot expand its partnership group fast enough and so must delegate more and more of the work to its less qualified associates. In that five-year period, the ratio of associates to partners rose from five to one to six to one. In the German branch, it rose to seven to one.[2]

Knowledge companies that grow organically are often governed by professional values (that is, they have professionals in power) rather than organizational values (that is, they have managers in power). To the leaders of such companies, volume growth is not an end in itself but merely a means of assuring growth of knowledge and the personal development and satisfaction of their fellow professionals.

MERGERS DON'T WORK

Organic growth is the safest kind of growth for the knowledge organization. The problem is that a growth rate of less than 15 percent is not enough to satisfy ambitious leaders, especially when they compare themselves with the heroes of enterprise featured on the front pages of business magazines. The ability to build and expand organizations rapidly is generally reckoned to be the prime criterion of management ability. Whether a growth rate of 10 percent is sufficient or not is therefore more a question of the individual manager's perspective.

Mergers often fail to work, and this is doubly true of knowledge organizations in which cultural conflicts abound. U.S. consulting firm Alexander Proudfoot almost went broke when it bought Indevo (after an unsuccessful attempt by Bain), once Sweden's largest management consulting firm. Indevo had already virtually committed suicide by trying to branch out into advertising and finance. McKinsey too has tried and failed to grow through mergers. In 1989 it bought the U.S. information technology systems consultant ICG. ICG's two hundred IT (information technology) professionals and McKinsey's then-fifteen hundred consultants collided head-on, and most of the ICG consultants quit.

For knowledge companies that want to grow faster than organic growth permits, merger and acquisition is really just a quick way to recruit large numbers of staff or to get at a stock of customers, as in the accounting business. WM-data and others have shown that a combination of organic and inorganic growth, that is, a healthy and profitable core business supplemented by a very selective acquisition strategy, is a feasible method of expanding at a rate of more than 15 percent a year.

◄ Being Large: Managing Pro-Teams

Most large companies lie somewhere between the archetypal knowledge organization and the industrialized service organization typified by McDonald's. A whole range of activities with varying knowledge content—from fully automated services to customized problem solving—may often be found in the same company.

Highly educated professionals form a small minority in most large service and manufacturing companies. They're in the R&D labs, planning departments, and design offices. Such departments are usually very different from the rest of the organization, and it is easy to tell by the way their members dress and act that they enjoy more freedom than those in the production area.

PROFESSIONAL VALUES DOMINATE

"The others envy those of us who work in the R&D department," says the development manager of Wallac, a Finnish instrument maker. "We don't punch time clocks, and we can come and go as we please. Some people resent that. But you can't be creative from nine to five!"

Since creativity, or inventiveness, is the measure of ability here, working in research confers higher status than working in development, so development engineers are usually aspiring researchers. People rarely move the other way, from research to development. Another possible career path for development engineers is to move into marketing, but their values are not always attuned to the job. "I was a salesman for eight months," a development engineer recalled, "but I got so fed up with all the lies I had to tell and the unethical attitude of my colleagues that I applied for a transfer back to the development department."

Those who work in these types of professional departments tend to see themselves as a class apart: more serious, more knowledgeable, a cut above the rest. They tend to form their own clubs and try to create their own cultures, sometimes expressed in undergraduate-type exuberance. In short, they behave like the stereotypical expert described in Chapter 5.

These groups or *pro-teams*—that is, cadres or teams of professionals within an organization—are in control of much of the most valuable intangible assets.[3] Because managers in large companies tend to be unaware of the particulars involved in managing professionals, they may either stifle them or inadvertently allow them too much freedom. However, pro-teams can be dealt with effectively in three ways: through *integration, outsourcing,* and *insourcing.*

INTEGRATION: DISSOLVING THE PRO-TEAM

Twenty years ago there were not as many professionals around. In addition, most of them were based at the head office, where they worked as part of what was called *the staff* in the military sense. Staffers were highly educated and spent their time writing reports and doing analyses. They gave expert advice to line managers and often played a gatekeeper function, preparing the material upon which the top management decisions were based. The real decision makers were the line managers. These people usually came up the career ladder the long way and were thus quite different from, and often deeply suspicious of, the staffers. To the line managers, the

staffers were just a bunch of highly educated and articulate inspec-
tors who swarmed around, giving advice without the benefit of any
contact with reality.

The conflict between line and staff was and still is one of the classic problems in organization theory. The staffers were actually *pro-
teams,* just as in any department where a number of professionals are
gathered together.

Highly educated engineers and MBAs are no longer a rarity and,
thus, the staffers have spread throughout most organizations. They
have been decentralized down to subsidiary levels and no longer
report directly to top management. Discussion of the line–staff problem in management has abated accordingly. One might say that the
solution to the line–staff problem was to integrate the pro–teams into
the rest of the organization; they no longer exist.

OUTSOURCING: FROM CINDERELLA TO KNOWLEDGE COMPANY

The beauty of outsourcing is that it can transform what was previously a peripheral, low–status service function within a large company into an independent mission–driven business that is based on
core competencies (Hamel and Prahalad 1990). With a wave of the
spin–off wand, the Cinderellas of industry—the gatekeepers, the night
watchmen, the cleaners, the caretakers—become security executives,
hygiene specialists, or building managers employed by small firms
for whom their experience and skills are vital assets.

Some dismiss such relabeling of roles as cosmetic, but they miss
the point entirely. The change in status from ancillary worker to
bearer of the core competence of the firm is profoundly significant
because it gives people self–respect. They begin to take pride in their
work and they become aware of a hunger they never felt when
employed by large firms to perfect and develop their skills. The
change in attitude occurs because they now see themselves differently. They can begin to reach outside their own organization for education, they can begin to relate to other people with similar jobs, they
can learn from the experts. The effect of all this is that the former
dependent worker becomes more of an independent professional.

This change in perspective affects strategy in a profound way.
When knowledge of cleaning is the core business, the skill of the
cleaners become a strategic core competence. The same magic works,
only more so, when the spun–off service has a larger expertise component. Each day, the outsourcing by large organizations of financial
management, accounting, data processing, consultants, specialized

maintenance, and so on is swelling the service sector ranks with scores of knowledge companies eager to sell their services to third parties as well as to their erstwhile employers.

Many of today's knowledge companies can trace their origins to large firms or universities. Major industrial groups like General Electric and leading universities and institutes of technology like Stanford, MIT, and Cambridge in the United Kingdom spawned thousands of such firms during the 1980s. A survey carried out by the Swedish Institute of Industrial Economics revealed that as much as two-thirds of the growth in the service sector during the 1972 to 1982 period was accounted for by spin-offs from industrial corporations. In fact, it seems that the rapid growth of knowledge companies can be explained by the trend among large industrial companies to focus more on their core technologies.

OUTSOURCING: CREATING A SEPARATE ENTITY

What do you do about awkward units that make demands of their own and can make their demands stick because they consist of irreplaceable experts? If they grow too troublesome, you can simply let them form their own company by outsourcing. Outsourcing is also frequently used in the public sector as a method to improve efficiency and the working conditions of valuable experts, who are otherwise lured away by the private sector. With outsourcing, professionals can manage their own affairs, set up their own rules, and be as awkward as they like or as successful as they can. The company's only remaining dealings with them are on a customer-supplier footing.

Such amicable and mutually respectful separations are usually beneficial to both parties. It is in the outsourced organization's interests to take great care of what at first may be its only customer, so the end result is often much better service than when the outsourced team was an in-house department. This was the route that *Affärsvärlden* chose when our financial database subsidiary wanted to pursue a different strategy. (See Chapter 10 for more on this.)

INSOURCING: CREATING A FIRM WITHIN THE FIRM

Sometimes relations between the pro-team and the rest of the organization become so strained that its members quit. This is usually a dramatic and often a traumatic experience for those involved. Relations are broken and re-formed. Sometimes the former parent will remain a customer but only if that is absolutely essential to the health of its own business. Soon, especially if the new organization starts competing with the old, the breach is total.

To keep the relationship sound, the pro–team may be retained as a firm within the firm, that is, as a subsidiary company or as a separate entity. This procedure may be called *insourcing* (Pinchot and Pinchot 1995). The new entity acquires its own identity and is at least partly isolated from the rest of the organization. It acquires its own management, its own profit–and–loss account, perhaps even its own balance sheet, and usually its own board of directors and managing director. This was a common method for controlling the growth of bureaucracy in large organizations during the 1980s.

However, insourcing is not a final solution because soon the management of the new company starts to get business from third parties, and when this business becomes a sizable part of the total, the subsidiary's managers begin to ask whether they need the security of the parental patronage. That's when the question of a management buyout crops up. Thus, companies that set up subsidiaries must be prepared for the time when the subsidiaries want to cut loose and go their own way. This is particularly dangerous if the firm within the firm sits on some of the core competencies.

BANKS: INSOURCING STOCKBROKERS

Most bank employees are occupied with fairly routine monetary transactions. A minority, only a small percent, work in the investment banking and brokering areas.

In 1983, the Swedish stock market began to take off and interest in investing exploded. This led to an acute shortage of people familiar with the stock market and share trading. In the banks, such people were to be found in a couple of obscure low–status departments: the securities department and the trustee department. When demand for their knowledge began to increase, they found that their market value outside the bank had suddenly risen to much more than they were currently being paid. When bank managements ignored their demands for salary increases, they defected in droves to the newly formed stockbrokerage firms that tempted them with convertible loan stock and other perks that the banks were unable to offer under the terms of their agreement with the bank employees' union.

The banks rapidly lost market share in the fast–growing, very lucrative brokerage market. In 1980 Swedish banks had a 61 percent share of the brokerage market, then worth 90 million Swedish kronor a year. But by 1985, their share was down to 43 percent of the 711 million kronor in brokerage fees paid that year. They later recouped some of their losses, but they never regained the 1980 level.

Thus bank managements were abruptly and forcefully made aware of the true value of this small group of employees, and after a few years they took steps to hold on to them. Salaries were raised, performance bonuses offered, and the old trustee departments converted into separate companies so that the preferential treatment they received would not cause too much discontent among the rest of the staff. So, in our terminology, the banks used insourcing to let their pro-teams loose while still keeping control over them.

Summary

- Although knowledge organizations make gains in marketing presence when they are larger, research suggests that size gives them no economies of scale in production; fifty employees seems a maximum for an organization or a work unit.
- More highly educated employees can lead to higher efficiency in publishing.
- Large corporations can be more efficient by splitting the company into pro-teams, that is, groups of professionals that cooperate within a framework of administration and marketing.
- Expert islands—that is, experts forming their own "clubs" and creating their own cultures—may cause problems in large companies. Solutions are integrating, outsourcing, and insourcing.
- A Swedish study shows that two-thirds of the growth of knowledge companies comes from outsourcing.

Advice to Managers

- Organic growth is a sign of a healthy organization. Acquisitions are risky and should be made to gain intangible assets, not to gain volume.
- The key to successful mergers and acquisitions lies in how the intangible assets are handled.
- It is important to be aware of the disadvantage of scale in creative work; groups of people should not exceed fifty in number.
- The invisible assembly lines built into an organization should be identified and dismantled in those areas where creativity is a requirement.

- Professional islands should be identified and their problems addressed; the problems tend to be in the interface with the mother organization.
- The company mission or business idea should be developed in close cooperation with the experts.
- By recruiting larger numbers of highly educated people, an organization will introduce forces that will move it toward knowledge organization status.
- Ideas only need to be sold to the experts; the others will follow.

Managing External Structures
to Maximize Knowledge Assets

To manage the external structure is to manage the external flows of knowledge in customer and supplier relationships. The management skills involve selling, public relations, marketing, and so on, which merit discussions beyond the scope of this book. Rather, this chapter and the next focus on strategies for increasing returns.

This chapter describes two strategies for managing external structures: the information-focused strategy and the knowledge-focused strategy. The two strategies build on the differences between information and knowledge and the characteristics of the markets for information and knowledge, as discussed earlier in the book. The two strategies will be compared in Chapter 10.

⚬ The Business of Information

Chapter 4 described the two basic methods of transferring knowledge between people: the indirect way through information and the direct, person-to-person way, the learning-by-doing way that I call tradition.

It is generally accepted that information is a valuable resource and that it is possible to improve decisions and reduce risk by gathering information. But the behavior of the financial information markets suggests the opposite.

THE LOW OR NEGATIVE VALUE OF INFORMATION
Information has been traded on the financial markets since the dawn of the mass media market in the early nineteenth century. Aided by new developments in computer technology like desktop publishing, the publishing industry has undergone a revolution that

has greatly increased the ease with which information is produced and led to a huge increase in the amount produced. As a result, financial market traders are now inundated with information in the form of tips, databases, newsletters, magazines, television and radio reports, and so on. By my reckoning (Sveiby 1994), the supply of information from the mass media that is of relevance to financial markets has grown at an exponential rate, by at least tenfold over the past ten years. But there is no evidence that this flood of information has improved the quality of investment decisions one jot. On the contrary, the past decade has witnessed the most disastrous misjudgments by professional economists and financial analysts since the Great Depression of the 1930s.

Figure 14 summarizes the market for business and financial information in Sweden today. The value added to the information is plotted on the vertical axis, and the time taken to convey it from the source to the reader, listener, or viewer is plotted on the horizontal axis.

One can distinguish three broad classes of value added and three broad spans of lead time. A rough categorization of the three levels of value added is the following:

- Level 1: Price figures only. No valued added.
- Level 2: News text. Some valued added.
- Level 3: Analysis. Much value added.

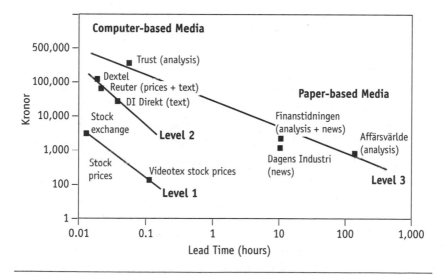

Figure 14. The market for financial information in Sweden, 1990. Source: Ph.D. thesis, Karl E. Sveiby.

Real–time media via computer have captured the market for the very fastest information. Broadcast media have become cheap channels for financial news and prices, with relatively low value added. Print media are represented in all three value–added levels and in all but the fastest time niches. Prices vary according to both time and value added. Codified and easily disseminated information (share prices, for example) has the lowest market value. The three value-added levels seem to describe a roughly logarithmic curve and are all strongly influenced by the time factor.

The cost of stock price information (Level 1) has fallen to the cost of transmitting the bit stream. Generally speaking, it seems to be worth no more than what it costs to retrieve it from computers. The price of such simple, coded information falls rapidly as it becomes more widely accessible. The price of plain news text (Level 2) is also falling fast because the longer the lead time, the cheaper information must be in order to find a market. The fall is slowest for information with the most value added (Level 3), but prices here are also time-sensitive. The faster media are growing, while the slower stagnate. If we have to choose between lead time and added value, we seem to choose lead time.

The media market is enjoying a boom in the mid–1990s, just as it did in the mid–1980s. This time, the boom is occurring mainly in the area of television and business and financial information aimed at investors. In Europe alone four new channels have been launched recently to broadcast business news and comment practically around the clock: European Business News, BBC World, Sky News, and CNBC Money Wheel.

Who pays for this information? Not the viewers because they get it free. These days, only special cable channels are bold enough to charge viewers for what they see. All the revenues are expected to come from advertisers. Most new print launches today are also freebies. Even established, prestigious papers with high subscription rates, like the *Financial Times*, earn 75 percent of their revenues from advertising.

The new computerized media offer open access to gigabytes of information stored in the databases of public networks free of charge. Except for some financial databases, once you have paid a fee to the gatekeeper, almost all the information is free. So the suppliers of information pay rather than the consumers, which is not at all the way one would expect the market for a valuable resource to behave.

What lesson does the modern mass media market teach us? Information is a commodity with a very short shelf life. After fifteen years in the information business, my conclusion is that it is getting harder and harder to charge for information. You can find plenty of people willing to give information away, but it is becoming increasingly difficult to find people willing to spend time reading what others have written or listening to what others have to say, let alone to spend money on it. Why? Because it takes time, experience, and mental effort to turn information into useful knowledge. And since recipients cannot know until afterward whether it was worth spending that time, information that turns out to be worthless is really worth less than nothing.

All modern information markets are characterized by an excess of supply over demand, and there is nothing to suggest this situation will change. On the contrary, information is becoming ever cheaper and easier to produce, while our capacity to absorb it increases only slowly as the quality of our education improves. The constraint nowadays is the time we have to read, watch, or listen—not a shortage of money. This is true of all kinds of articulated knowledge, whether packaged as books, newspapers, films, television and radio programs, databases, or multimedia shows.

LESS INFORMED WITH MORE INFORMATION

What is the result of this oversupply of information and our limited time to digest it? When you can pick and choose information, there is always some authority that will support a particular view. So what is the point in collecting any information at all? Is a chaos of information better than none at all? Increasingly, we cut it off. We read catchy headlines rather than the whole story. We buy stock on the strength of "tips" rather than on the basis of a thorough analysis we have made ourselves.

This leads to a curious paradox. Although we have access to more information than ever before, we have become more and more dependent on the subjective opinions of those who filter information. The subjective opinions of editors, for example, decide what should be plucked from the information chaos to become "news." In such a frenetic atmosphere only the best-known people and the most extravagant statements get heard. An ill-founded opinion spoken loosely by a celebrity gets far more attention than a hundred-page report covering an issue from all angles.

INFORMATIZED MARKETS: FASTER, RISKIER, COSTLIER

Nicholas Leeson's sour half-grin at the cameras during his forced return to Europe has become a symbol of the horrendous risks that are run in the financial derivatives market. Some investment bankers insisted that the $1 billion Barings Bank disaster was one of a kind and that their systems would prevent it from happening again. But then there was the Daiwa security trader who caused a $1.1 billion loss, and then there was a Sumitomo copper trader who caused a $2 billion loss. One wonders whether the erstwhile leaders of Barings really understood the kind of business they were getting the Queen's investment bank into when they let Leeson loose in Singapore.

In less than ten years the professional financial markets have become the most information–intensive business environment in the world. They exemplify, for better or worse, what we can expect in other markets when information in computer networks replaces physical goods and transactions.

The physical products of financial markets—coins, notes, and securities—have now been largely replaced by information on computer disks. Physical transportation of money is becoming increasingly rare; money is moved between computers in the form of information. An electronic marketplace has replaced the physical stock exchange floor; brokers only "see" their counterparts as names on computer screens.

The first thing one notices when an environment becomes so highly *informatized*—as I call it—is that the speed of transaction accelerates sharply. Financial markets have now reached the stage where human reaction times are too slow for people to do business themselves. More and more deals are done by computer systems in programmed trading. Electronic document transfers and automatic billing are becoming common in other industries, too.

The second thing one notices about such markets is that prices fluctuate far more than they used to. This is most obvious in the financial markets, but commodity markets are also more volatile than they were, and shares in information–related companies like software firms also fluctuate more than other shares.[1]

Financial derivatives and other so–called futures have been invented to manage the higher risks. When one deals in derivatives, one buys or sells the change in the price of a share or a ton of copper, not the commodity itself. Financial derivatives are pure information. They were designed to afford protection to investors, but it turns out that the derivatives market is the riskiest of all, as the fate of Barings Bank so glaringly demonstrates. Derivatives and other futures contracts have turned out not to be concentrations of risk that reduce risk elsewhere but additional packages of information that have increased the risk of the whole market.

The third distinctive quality of highly informatized markets is the huge sums operators invest in computers and computer systems and the conspicuous absence of any discernible returns from their investments. There is no evidence that the computerization of financial markets has lowered risk or increased returns. Despite being supported by infinitely more information, investment decisions are as good or as bad as they were before the computer era.

No financial market firm has derived a lasting competitive advantage from its computers. Information and the instruments or programs designed to handle it spread like wildfire, but the main effect on the players of informatizing these markets may be likened to the act of obeying the Red Queen in *Alice in Wonderland*: running faster and faster just to stay in the same place.

LESSONS TO BE LEARNED

When thinking about information markets in everyday terms, one sees mostly paradoxes:

- In information markets suppliers pay, not consumers. Thus, far from being a valuable resource, information often has a negative value.
- When a market becomes informatized, the risks increase so the commercial value of the goods falls.
- Time, not money, is the currency on informatized markets.
- The speed of delivery is more important than content.
- Adding information tends to obscure, rather than clarify.
- Subjective opinions are more valuable than objective facts.
- The main effect of informatizing a market is to oblige the players to run faster just to stay in the same place.

There is no doubt that informatized markets are strange and dangerous places. Selling information does not seem like a good business. So who makes the money?

Making Money in the Information Markets

How is money made in the informatized markets? Likely, it is that which becomes the standard for information suppliers, like Microsoft, or the major television channel, like that owned by Rupert Murdoch, or the tools for the suppliers of information, like Netscape. When Bill Gates and IBM signed their historic 1983 agreement to make MS–DOS the operating system for IBM's new PC, neither could foresee just how valuable the deal would turn out to be for Microsoft. MS–DOS was not then and by some accounts is not now the best operating system available, but because IBM allowed Microsoft to sell it to all PC makers it became the de facto standard and thus the environment within which all software developers were obliged to design their applications.

In this way, MS–DOS writes the rules for knowledge creation in the PC world, and Microsoft makes money from end users who are stuck with its operating system, whether they like it or not. As we will see in the next section, Netscape Communications has created a new strategic archetype for addressing information markets based on the apparently bizarre principle of giving away its Internet browser to anyone who wants it. Netscape makes its money from its servers, that is, from the advertisers on the Internet. Microsoft Network (Microsoft's Internet subsidiary) has belatedly realized the logic of information markets and abandoned its original plan of locking content providers into its Web software and charging fees in favor of a similar strategy—allowing the use of any browser, slashing content prices, and getting revenues from on-line advertisers instead.

The flurry of merger activity in the media industry has been inspired by the desire of the big players to grab as large a share as they can of the television and video distribution channels. They see the framework within which the multimedia industry operates and develops as more valuable than its content. Some still insist that, in the end, content is king, but all the evidence so far suggests that in this strange fledgling industry it is the rule setters who make the increasing returns, not the content providers, and that those who use the new superhighways as communications media are more likely to benefit commercially than those who see information as a product.

NETSCAPE: WINNING IN INFORMATION MARKETS

In August 1995 Netscape Communications went public in one of the most oversubscribed initial public offerings in history. A company with a mere $16 million in revenues and negligible profits ended its first day of public trading with a market value of $2 billion. Its tangible net worth is minuscule, so the value of Netscape is entirely intangible.

The firm is best known for its Netscape Navigator Web browser, a kind of "reading glass" for the Internet. A browser like Navigator creates a graphical interface for computers linked to the World Wide

Web via the Internet. It is possible to read Internet files without browsers, but the information is displayed as lines of text, with no headings, graphics, or colors.

Computer wizard Marc Andreesen, cofounder of Netscape, created the first such interface—Mosaic—in the winter of 1993 when he was twenty-three years old. In accordance with the Net culture, Mosaic was distributed as "freeware," which costs nothing to download. According to one of Andreesen's colleagues, Mosaic was not a very good browser, but it was the first. Distribution via the Internet was rapid. Within a year of Mosaic's launch, three million people were using it.

Netscape makes no secret of its wish to dominate the Internet market, but its strategy defies conventional wisdom. How can a company that gives its products away dominate a market in a commercial sense? Netscape makes its money from its servers—software run by a host computer that allows other computers to connect to it. Its servers are graphic and are, of course, optimized for its own Web browser. It is a bit like ordinary publishing. Web servers host the information on the Internet as "pages" and "print" them on our computer screens via the browsers. By giving Mosaic away, Netscape created enormous pull from its users. Other software firms soon developed browsers that were better than Mosaic, but because Mosaic was the first, it had the largest number of copies and thus still created the greatest pull.

After a frenzy of coding—some programmers had to work 130 hours a week—Netscape launched its first commercial Web browser in the winter of 1994 as shareware. In other words, it was free to download, but you were asked to send $10 or $20 to Netscape if you liked it. If you didn't, you were not punished.

Netscape's Navigator has rapidly become the de facto Internet standard just as Microsoft's MS–DOS operating system became the PC standard. Now that its market share is established, Netscape is no longer giving it away but charges a small amount.

Netscape created an essential tool for using the Web, but the Web is also the market (there would be no Netscape if there were no Web) the marketing tool (new versions of the Navigator program are advertised on Netscape's home page) and the distribution channel (users download the software straight from Netscape's home page). If you are not happy with the program, if you detect a bug, or if you would like a new feature, you e-mail the creator and get a reply within minutes—at least in theory. Netscape receives so much customer feedback that its e-mail box is always clogged, but more than enough feedback gets through to enable Netscape systems engineers to improve the software continually in response to customer wishes.

It is not a critical problem for Netscape if users of the Web browser do not pay a lot. The revenues come from companies who want to reach those who use the browsers. These customers buy the servers, are invoiced by Netscape, and pay through the traditional channels, in the normal way.

NETSCAPE VERSUS MICROSOFT

When Microsoft launched Windows 95 on August 24, 1995, it was the culmination of an enormous effort. The beta version had been mailed to some four hundred thousand people the previous February to test for bugs. The final coding was done in June, but it took another two months to organize ten manufacturing plants to make the CD–ROMs, print two million manuals, pack them up with the CD–ROMs, and then ship them on five hundred trucks to twenty thousand outlets in the United States.

The timing was critical because everything had to coincide with a $250 million advertising campaign—the largest in the history of the computer industry. Managers then had to wait several weeks for the first feedback from retailers and customers. It was an extraordinary exercise. It had required Microsoft's six thousand employees to push themselves to the limit for a year or more, it had cost a bundle, and it was rightly hailed as a major management triumph.

In contrast, Netscape's retail distribution to millions of customers takes minutes, not months. Few people are involved, apart from the programmers and the customers, and no management is needed to organize the distribution; there are no printers, trucks, or retail outlets, just modems and telephone lines. And it doesn't cost much either. Netscape's three hundred employees can reach as many customers in minutes as Microsoft's six thousand employees can in months, and for an infinitesimal fraction of the cost. With comparisons like these, it is no wonder that Bill Gates felt obliged to announce a new Internet strategy for Microsoft at the end of 1995.

By good luck or by good judgment, Netscape has stumbled on a winning strategy for information markets. Revenues in information markets come from the sellers of information (that is, the advertisers) not from the buyers (that is, the readers). Thus, with Netscape's strategy, users of the reading tool—the Web browser—pay little or nothing. Netscape's strategy is analogous to that employed in publishing, where advertisers provide up to 100 percent of the total revenues of magazines and newspapers.

But customers in information markets do seem to be willing to pay for software that helps them to reduce information chaos, like graphical interfaces, and "engines" that search the Web. Netscape doesn't sell information in the form of facts but in the form of tools, tools for sifting, selecting, and otherwise reducing the information maze of the World Wide Web.

LESSONS TO BE LEARNED

Two maxims are widely accepted by the markets for high-tech products: it pays to be the first and it pays to have superb technology. In these respects Netscape's strategy resembles Microsoft's. But Netscape gave its first product away and won a 70 percent market share. The company achieved Microsoftlike dominance in its market within months by being exceedingly aggressive.

High-tech industries have also taught us the value of entertaining close relations with selected customers who can challenge your people and provide you with qualified feedback. Netscape has compressed the time required to receive and test feedback. Their relations with some of the opinion-leader hackers on the Internet are close and intense, practically in real time, and this keeps them ahead of the competition.

Unlike Microsoft, Netscape has negligible retail distribution because most business is via the Net. No wonder Bill Gates fears it. Netscape is a turbo-charged Microsoft.

These examples show what characterizes an information-focused strategy: a low degree of customization, knowledge sold as a derivative, increasing returns from efficiency, large volumes and mass markets, investments in computer technology, and consideration of people as costs.

▪" A Knowledge-Focused Strategy

An information-focused strategy generates some intangible revenues from consumers, such as product feedback in the case of Netscape. But a knowledge-focused strategy generates a wider range of intangible revenues, and this is one of the principal differences between the two strategies.

THE CUSTOMER: THE SOURCE OF INTANGIBLE RETURNS

As Figure 15 shows, most customers are sources of value in forms other than hard cash.

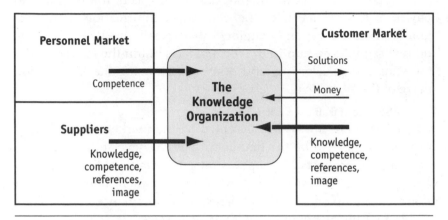

Figure 15. Intangible revenues from customers, new recruits, and suppliers.

Customers provide training for employees; they can be used as references; they talk to one another and so spread the word and an organization's image; and they encourage the development of competence with their demands. The knowledge company's choice of customers, therefore, is of vital strategic significance because the kind of customers a knowledge company works for determines both the quality and quantity of its intangible knowledge revenues. Furthermore, ultimately the flow of knowledge from customers will become a source of visible revenue.

As Exhibit 4 shows, intangible revenues can be classified among the three types of intangible assets.

Thus, customers are especially important to knowledge organizations. The big auditing firms, for example, use their large customers to train new recruits by assigning them the routine parts of the audit. That such customers are valuable is recognized by the senior auditors and the large customers. Indeed, the latter are asking with increasing frequency these days what they will get in return for teaching their auditor–rookies their business.

Other customers contribute their image. Having IBM or General Motors as a customer is a valuable reference, and it is quite remarkable how many big–name companies appear as existing or former clients on a consultant's curriculum vitae. However, the size of the customer has little to do with how interesting or challenging the pro-

Improving the external structure (customer relations)	Improving the internal structure	Improving the competence of people
Referrals of new customers (reducing sales and marketing costs)	Leverage of R&D projects (when solutions developed for one customer are reused)	Learning (on-the-job training)
Prestige (making it easier to sell and recruit personnel)	Projects that support knowledge transfer (reducing dependency on individuals)	Ideas (for new products or services)

Exhibit 4. There are three kinds of invisible revenues: those that improve customer relations, those that improve the internal structure, and those that improve competence.

jects are. The most challenging and therefore the most educational work is often done for less well-known customers. A knowledge-focused strategy therefore involves getting to know one's customers well.

When armed with an intimate understanding of its customers, a knowledge company can be more selective in its marketing and can concentrate its most valuable (that is, its scarcest) skills on projects where they fit best and will do the most good for both the customer and the knowledge company itself.

The fact that a small country like Sweden boasts such a large and successful communications company as Ericsson is largely attributable to the fact that Ericsson has been and is still being driven to develop its knowledge by a knowledgeable and demanding customer: Telia, the former Swedish Telecom Service. Supporting this point of view, Michael Porter (1980) argues that the existence or absence of demanding customers helps explain why some national industries become globally competitive while others do not.

Most knowledge companies use customer projects to develop new methods and, as anyone who has worked in sales will tell you, projects undertaken successfully for high-profile customers are, irrespective of their profitability, invaluable aids in selling because they attract attention and can be used as reference accounts for years afterwards.

ꞏꞏ McKinsey & Company: Winning with a Knowledge-Focused Strategy

How does a knowledge-focused strategy generate intangible revenues for companies? As illustrated by the consulting firm McKinsey, a knowledge-focused strategy creates a relationship with the customer that is very different from an information-focused strategy. This example demonstrates how to leverage intangible assets.

With some $1.7 billion in billings in 1995 and six thousand employees, McKinsey is not the largest consulting firm in the world, but it is among the most profitable and may even be said to have the best image worldwide. It is also one of the oldest. It was founded in 1922 by the lawyer James O. McKinsey, although the leadership was soon assumed by Marvin Bower. McKinsey has come a long way since the 1970s, when it was best known for its cost-cutting skills. Today, it advises many of the world's largest companies on strategy and organizational change, and its continuing success is the envy of its rivals.

The firm is built on individual competence, so its strategy starts with recruitment. McKinsey hires the best and the brightest from top universities and business schools. Some 80 percent of its recruits are twenty-nine years old or younger, either fresh from university or with limited experience. In order to get to know its potential employees as well as possible before approaching them, McKinsey recruiters are in close contact with the schools, on the lookout for intellectual and analytical ability.

Some 15 percent of applicants to McKinsey are interviewed by senior partners who have to decide whether they want the interviewees on their teams. About 20 percent of those interviewed (3 percent of applicants) receive an offer. Freshmen are immediately thrown in at the deep end on client work acting as "grinders": searching databases and analyzing enormous amounts of information. McKinsey's database of assignment reports and its global computer network have become essential tools in this task. New employees feel they are immediately involved in important matters because the report they generate is the cornerstone of a McKinsey assignment. Young, ambitious new employees are further drilled in the firm's guiding principles and the *Perspectives on McKinsey*, a three-hundred-page bible written by the legendary Marvin Bower. They are encouraged to socialize with each other and are often invited to parties held by senior partners.

After the first assignments, it is up or out. At annual engagement performance reviews, people either advance to become one of the firm's five hundred partners or are asked to leave the firm. But McKinsey takes care of its alumni. It tries to find them good jobs; it even runs an alumni club. In this way, it maintains good relations with people who might later become valued clients.

McKinsey is aware of the danger that its strong and demanding culture will stifle creativity and tries to counter the risk by using Bower's credo, *obligation to dissent,* which insists that all be allowed to speak their minds no matter their rank. The firm also encourages partners to do R&D and write books, but only if doing so helps with client work. Some find this stipulation hard to comply with. Tom Peters, for example, was ousted from the partnership when his appetite for the limelight was seen to be interfering with his devotion to clients. The rule at McKinsey is that the client comes first, then the firm, and last the individual. Senior McKinsey partners are the client "finders and minders." They spend a lot of their time talking to clients and advising them, which they often do not charge for. In this way they maintain close personal relationships in the hopes that they will lead to large assignments later on.

McKinsey's assignments are carried out by teams of five, each led by a senior partner. The firm bills for teams rather than individuals; it charges high rates for inexperienced juniors. Annual revenue per consultant is close to $500,000. Clients are willing to pay these rates because they know the juniors have access to a large toolbox of methods, techniques, and ideas developed by top McKinsey consultants. In other words, even the lowliest McKinsey associate functions within a framework of knowledge accumulated by previous generations.

McKinsey does not employ traditional marketing methods; it "sells" by endeavoring to become so attractive that customers come knocking on their own.[2] Traditional selling and marketing activities are of limited value, McKinsey believes. The method is rather to volunteer one's knowledge and entertain the relationships so that customers want to return. When the consultants have completed an assignment, they have, together with their client's managers, created new knowledge that improves both the client's performance and McKinsey's knowledge base. But knowledge is not all that McKinsey offers. Sometimes the firm is called in to validate decisions clients have already made. Nothing is more persuasive in a strategy debate than the report of a McKinsey investigation. In these situations, McKinsey sells information that, based on its reputation and image, is regarded as valuable. The client pays for uniqueness, but a copy of the information in the report is, of course, retained in the McKinsey database.

LESSONS TO BE LEARNED

The McKinsey approach reads like a to-do list for increasing returns with a knowledge-focused strategy. Each action in Exhibit 5 establishes links to knowledge creation and creates intangible revenues that improve internal and external structures.

McKinsey proves that it is possible to convert the invisible knowledge flows from all these activities into tangible and visible money revenues. McKinsey also shows the multitude of opportunities to create invisible revenues.

▪ A Runner-Up's Use of a Knowledge-Focused Strategy

The runners-up in information markets face formidable odds. The case history of the Swedish business magazines *Affärsvärlden* (AFV) and *Veckans Affärer* (VA)—already mentioned in Chapter 8—illustrates how competitive position can improve when the runner-up initiates a knowledge-focused strategy.

Initially, AFV was a David challenging a Goliath. In 1975 AFV had six journalists and sales of 5 million kronor, whereas VA had thirty journalists and revenues of 25 million kronor. Figure 16 shows the difference in the number of printed pages.

There are substantial advantages of scale in the printing process because loading the press with plates and paper and adjusting it represents a large fixed cost; after that, the marginal cost of printing one page is no more than maybe 10 percent of the average cost. Thus the larger the print run, the lower the cost per page. The leverage is not as extreme as copying a computer disk, but not that different.

The economies of scale and the difference in pages had an obvious outcome: in 1983–84, one of VA's 204 million full-color pages cost 8.5 öre (Swedish cents) to print while one of AFV's 73 million pages cost 11.9 öre. This represented a cost handicap of nearly 30 percent for AFV (even though its pages contained only half as much full-color print as VA's) or a full 2 million kronor. Despite falling production costs for both magazines and rising volume for AFV, the gap remained throughout the decade.

Action	Link to knowledge creation and creation of intangible revenues
Carefully select bright young people who are easy to indoctrinate.	This creates inflow of new fresh competence eager to learn.
Provide "up-or-out" career paths; do not allow plateaus.	Individuals are encouraged to maintain steep learning curve or leave; this also creates necessary turnover.
Maintain "one-firm" concept (strong cultural indoctrination).	This creates strong tradition that improves knowledge conversion.
Use juniors as "grinders."	This enables tradition of tacit knowledge.
Put clients first, the firm second, the consultant last.	This code of ethics gives focus and purpose to knowledge creation.
Build close personal relations with a few selected clients.	Good chemistry leads to references, industry update, perhaps the next assignment.
Treat image as an important asset.	This reduces marketing costs.
Let young learn from old in master-apprentice relationships.	This enables tradition of tacit knowledge.
Treat former employees as honored alumni.	Instead of creating enemies that might reduce image, retained relationships may turn into new clients.
Go for the large assignments that allow teams.	Teams allow tradition of tacit knowledge among members.
Develop own consulting concepts.	Creation of new knowledge equals R&D.
Publicize the concepts in books and seminars.	This influences the mindsets of potential customers; creates standards.
Focus on clients rather than markets.	Knowledge flows through relations, not through markets.
Create information-sharing system.	This supports knowledge combination.
Charge for teams, not for individuals.	This conceals the elevated fees of the seniors.

Exhibit 5. McKinsey's knowledge-focused strategy.

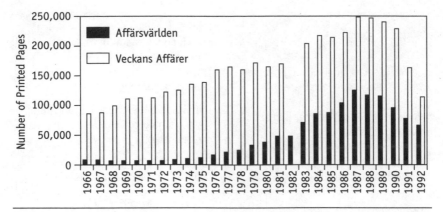

Figure 16. In the 1960s and 1970s, Veckans Affärer *printed six times as many pages as* Affärsvärlden. *Toward the end of the 1980s the difference had shrunk to two times as many.*

The cost advantage enjoyed by a larger paper enables it to hire good journalists and maintain a higher overall level of editorial quality. This can be the ticket to a virtuous circle of more readers, who provide more resources, which enable better quality, which attracts more readers, and so on and on. Even if the smaller magazine keeps lower prices, the larger and—for the magazine—more profitable advertisers prefer to place their ads in the large magazine because it gives them access to a larger audience. Publishers know that once established, the largest newspaper or magazine in a market is a license to print money. The runner-up AFV thus faced a formidable competitive barrier. It had no alternative but to try a different strategy than VA. What it did was to adopt a more knowledge-focused strategy.

AFV's journalists managed to produce many more pages per journalist than VA's (133 pages compared with VA's 62 in 1983–84). They also drew lower salaries, at least during the early 1980s. AFV thus managed to keep its editorial cost per page as low as 7.9 öre per page compared with VA's 13.7 öre. This difference in editorial productivity was sustained throughout the period even though absolute productivity declined in both cases: in 1990 AFV's journalists had an annual output of 114 pages compared with VA's 54. AFV, however, proved the value of its strategy by being more profitable than VA the whole period, as shown in Figure 17.

The profit margins of both magazines reached their peaks during the boom years 1980 to 1986, with levels of over 30 percent for AFV and 20 percent to 25 percent for VA. The new business daily

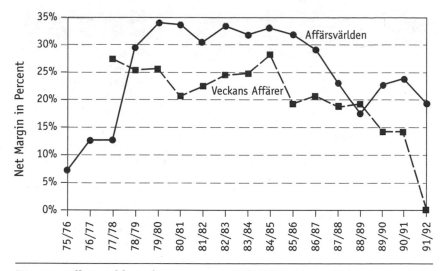

Figure 17. Affärsvärlden's *focus on managing the intangibles enabled it to maintain a higher profitability than* Veckans Affärer *during most of the period.*

Dagens Industri, launched at the end of the 1980s by the owner of VA, gradually began to displace both weeklies from the advertisement market and the good times were over.

When the economic recession of the 1990s hit the Swedish financial markets, both magazines came under heavy pressure. VA was hardest hit because its editorial concept involved high fixed costs. AFV had lower fixed costs and a more flexible concept; it allowed the editorial staff to work shorter hours without compensation, for example. The magazine was thus able to adjust rapidly by reducing the number of pages and cutting its fixed costs. AFV continued to operate at a profit while VA went into the red.

Veckans Affärer's problems caused its publishers to decide in March 1994 to split it into two journals: a smaller, cheaper weekly with a different concept and a more expensive monthly. In contrast, *Affärsvärlden* stuck to the niche strategy that had been its hallmark ever since it was relaunched in 1975. In 1994 it succeeded in regaining some of the lost volume and its circulation rose by almost 15 percent to 23,700 while circulation of *Veckans Affärer's* relaunched weekly remained unchanged at 33,800. *Affärsvärlden* continues to be one of the most profitable journals on the Swedish market.

The runner-up won its fight but the journal's owners lost the battle. After eighteen years of singleminded head-on competition, AFV had forced the leader to move out. But by then the leader's owner

Affärsvärlden's management actions	Link to knowledge creation and creation of intangible revenues	The common wisdom in Swedish publishing in the 1980s
Recruit analytical people from university and teach them to write.	Creates inflow of superior analytical competence.	Established (nonacademic) journalists are recruited and taught financial analysis.
Keep people from leaving by offering partnership.	Competence is not lost to competition.	No partnership is offered.
Put no by-lines on articles.	Reduces internal competition and enables knowledge sharing.	By-lines put on all articles.
Organize other departments like the open-space editorial room.	Enables tradition of tacit knowledge.	Only journalists sit in open-space offices.
Write articles in teams.	Enables tradition of tacit knowledge.	Articles written by individuals.
Journalistic ethic guides whole business.	Gives focus and purpose of knowledge creation.	Similar action taken.
Build close personal relations with Sweden's large companies.	Good chemistry leads to references, industry update, perhaps more subscriptions and ads.	Similar action taken.
Nurture image as "Sweden's most competent financial analysts" by giving seminars, etc.	Reduces marketing costs.	Similar action taken.
Treat former employees as honored alumni.	Instead of creating enemies that might damage image, relationships are retained and alumni can become new clients.	Not done.
Develop analytical concepts.	Creates new knowledge unique to the publication.	Not done.
Publicize the concepts in books and seminars.	Influences the mindsets of potential customers; creates standards.	Not done.
Focus on customers rather than markets.	Knowledge flows through relations not through markets.	Similar action taken.

Exhibit 6. Affärsvärlden's *knowledge-focused strategy.*

had already established the next wave—business dailies—which in terms of volume and profitability overtook them both.

AFFÄRSVÄRLDEN'S KNOWLEDGE-FOCUSED STRATEGY

Publishing companies are generally not regarded as knowledge organizations, but this case history illustrates how a knowledge-focused strategy can be successful in any industry. *Affärsvärlden* was involved in traditional print media, software, and consulting, so the dilemmas of choice between an information focus and a knowledge focus are also exposed.

A summary of the knowledge–focused strategy employed by *Affärsvärlden* during the 1980s is shown in Exhibit 6. This strategy gave the magazine a distinct competitive advantage in the market for financial information. The strategy went against the common sense of publishing, but its success created imitators among other journals and publishers in Sweden.

LESSONS TO BE LEARNED

A knowledge focused strategy can be very competitive, particu larly when it breaks with common sense. By leveraging its intangible assets, a runner–up can be more profitable than the market leader even in an information market; this phenomenon would otherwise be an anomaly.

Summary

- To manage the external structure is to manage the external flows of knowledge in customer and supplier relationships. There are two strategies for managing the external structure: information-focused and knowledge–focused.

- Information takes time and effort to read and digest. Therefore, information that turns out to be useless is really worth less than nothing.

- Adding information tends to obscure rather than clarify. Subjective opinions are more valuable than objective facts.

- Information markets have several unique characteristics. *Oversupply* reduces the value of information to a low or negative level. There is *acceleration* of the speed of transaction and price volatility. *Suppliers pay,* not consumers. *Speed of delivery is more important* than content. Money is made by those who *create the standard* for information suppliers, *own the major distribution channel,* or *sell tools to the suppliers* of information.

- An information-focused strategy earns increasing returns primarily by adapting to the development of information technology: offering a low degree of customization, aiming at mass markets, and exploiting low production cost of copying software. People are regarded as costs.
- A knowledge-focused strategy earns increasing returns primarily from intangible assets, assets that convert invisible revenues from a large number of activities into tangible revenues. People are regarded as revenues.
- Most customers bring intangible revenues by improving customer relations, the internal structure, or the competence of employees.
- In a knowledge-focused strategy, there is a high degree of customization, and knowledge is sold as a process.
- A knowledge-focused strategy can be very competitive, particularly when it breaks with common sense.

Advice to Managers

- Companies compete in two markets: for people and for customers. It is essential to create an explicit strategy for the personnel market that is linked to the strategy for the customer market.
- Time should be seen as the true competitive factor. If one company can run faster than the competition, it may become the winner that takes all.
- Beware informatized markets! They do not behave like more traditional markets.
- Companies should be knowledge-focused rather than information-focused.
- It is important to select customers with intangible revenues in mind. The most valuable revenue from customers is not money but knowledge.
- Competitors need to think twice before entering an information market and be careful to identify the leader's advantage or, even better, wait for the next technology wave.
- Knowledge companies should try to make themselves attractive by offering some of their knowledge in explicit form free of charge. Knowledge grows from sharing. When clients get some of a company's knowledge, they come back for more!

10
Comparing Knowledge-Focused and Information-Focused Strategies

The stories of Netscape, Microsoft, and *Affärsvärlden* demonstrate how to win in markets for knowledge derivatives. The stories of McKinsey and Saatchi & Saatchi, respectively, show how to win and lose in the market for knowledge as a problem-solving tool. All five of these companies compete for bright young people who can learn fast and are willing to work long hours. Such people are always in demand and, therefore, always in short supply, so they need to be treated accordingly—as if they were customers. All of these companies have developed distinctive cultures with strong, internal structures. Knowledge creation is the core production process. Netscape and, particularly, McKinsey cultivate very close customer relations.

But there is a key difference between them. Saatchi & Saatchi and McKinsey's businesses involve problem solving, whereas Netscape, Microsoft, and *Affärsvärlden* all package the knowledge of their people into *knowledge derivatives*, which are then sold as information products. All five firms can, with some stretching of the label, be called knowledge organizations, but only McKinsey and *Affärsvärlden* pursue something that can properly be called a knowledge-focused strategy. Microsoft and Netscape pursue information-focused strategies. Exhibit 7 summarizes the differences between the two strategies.

A knowledge-focused strategy earns increasing returns primarily from intangible assets. An information-focused strategy earns increasing returns primarily from adapting to information technology developments. As discussed earlier, knowledge companies compete in two markets—for customers and for personnel—so they need

Information-Focused Strategy	Knowledge-Focused Strategy
• Low degree of customization • Knowledge sold as derivative • Increasing returns from efficiency • Economy-of-scale advantages in production • Large volume and mass market • Investment in computer technology • People are seen as costs	• High degree of customization • Knowledge sold as process • Increasing returns from effectiveness • Economy-of-scale disadvantages in production • Small volume and individual clients • Investment in people • People are seen as revenues

Exhibit 7. *The two strategic focuses: information and knowledge.*

two strategies: one for attracting and keeping customers and another for attracting and keeping key people.

⫶ Grey Advertising: The Failure of an Information-Focused Strategy

Observera–Grey, the Swedish subsidiary of the U.S. advertising group Grey, had a quality problem. The work of an advertising agency is not confined to major campaigns requiring great creativity. Much of its business consists of producing attractive but simple leaflets, brochures, price lists, and so on. The creative stars of the profession dislike this work because it's monotonous. Moreover, ad agencies cannot bill the same high hourly fees for simple price lists as they can for major campaigns. As a result, employees assigned to these simpler tasks tend to be low in the organizational pecking order and to regard themselves as inferior. The forces of professional motivation make this situation almost inevitable. As a result of this kind of thing, Observera–Grey found it hard to maintain high quality in such assignments even when it put its best people to work on them. It was a dilemma that the agency wanted badly to solve.

Could information technology offer a solution? Observera–Grey set up an agency within the agency, a new small–job pro–team whose mission it was to produce straightforward advertising material but with the Observera–Grey hallmark of quality. Accomplishing this mission successfully would mean standardizing production to a degree that was unthinkable in the creative shop and boosting efficiency with the help of new computer technology. A different cat-egory of person was recruited and a special business manager appointed. The two pro-teams worked side by side and were soon competing according to the only reasonable criterion: who could solve customers' problems best.

The solution seemed straightforward and logical. But the com-puter technology developed so fast that the volume of business gen-erated by Observera-Grey's small-job pro-team was not enough to fund the almost monthly upgradings in computer technology demanded by the new information technology (IT) people. The old agency advertising professionals aggravated the problem by not being able to communicate with the new IT-proficient professionals; professionals coming from two such different backgrounds often have difficulties communicating with each other.

The money the computers consumed made Observera-Grey's next decision easy: it allowed the small-job pro-team to outsource itself. Since shrinking back to its creative core, Observera-Grey has once again become one of Sweden's most profitable advertising agencies.

LESSONS TO BE LEARNED

Advertising agencies normally pursue knowledge-focused strategies, and so does Grey. The failure at Grey was the result of management underestimating the problems of introducing an information-focused strategy into the same organization. Because the two strategies are so different, it is hard to shift from one to the other. The two strategies demand different kinds of investments. The pro-fessional traditions are very different too. Grey's management encountered the all-too-familiar problem of two professional tradi-tions not being able to communicate with each other. The managers had the respect of the advertising experts but they knew nothing about IT, so the IT professionals did not accept them.

The dilemma of choice between a knowledge-focused and an information-focused strategy is likely to be one that challenges most knowledge organizations in the future. The following case study exemplifies such a challenge. The case also shows the conflict between the advocates of these two strategies: the managers/admin-istrators who favor an information-focused strategy (and the use of information technology) in order to reduce costs and the profession-als who favor a knowledge-focused strategy in order to generate more revenue from customers and leverage their other intangible assets.

▪️ *Affärsvärlden:* Dilemma of Choice

The modern history of the Swedish business magazine *Affärsvärlden* dates back to 1975, when five journalists teamed up to take over the management and later the ownership of the firm.[1] The firm's development into a broad information company was inspired by the competencies and inclinations of its founders who, generally speaking, were of two kinds: people with a desire and an ability to run a company and people with a desire and an ability to analyze information and write articles. Thus, both organizational and professional skills were available right from the start, which is probably the main reason why the company has done so well. However, because there were two kinds of people involved, two tracks for expanding the business developed. The two tracks are shown in Figure 18.

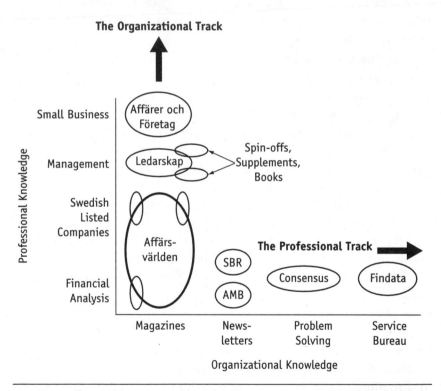

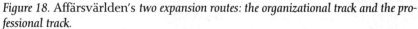

Figure 18. Affärsvärlden's *two expansion routes: the organizational track and the professional track.*

THE PROFESSIONAL TRACK

The professional expansion track was born when a few of the journal's leading analysts began to exploit their financial analyst skills by taking on consultancy projects. Initially, they framed a mission for the new business that was closely linked to that of *Affärsvärlden*. But before long the new subsidiary was caught in the explosive demand for financial analysis expertise. It became much more successful than anyone had expected, and its interests began to diverge from those of the parent company.

After a few years, the managers of the subsidiary wanted to branch out into the stockbrokerage business. The firm's leaders faced an ethical dilemma. It would be awkward to own both a business magazine and a stockbrokerage firm—there would be clear conflicts of interest when the magazine had to express views on the performance of the subsidiary's clients—so management decided to sell it.

Findata, an unrelated venture, began as a digital financial information database set up by the Stockholm School of Economics in the early 1970s. It started to collaborate on projects with *Affärsvärlden*, and in 1983 *Affärsvärlden*, Findata staff, and the school set up a joint company to commercialize the database. The combination of data and financial analysis was rare in Sweden at the time so there was a shortage of computer expertise when the financial markets took off in the early 1980s. Findata soon developed the character of a service agency, and its interest in providing the kind of financial analysis required by *Affärsvärlden* declined. As more and more of the common ground eroded, friction developed between Findata and *Affärsvärlden*, and Findata employees were allowed to buy the company in 1988. (It is now called Dextel-Findata and is owned by the publishing house Marieberg.)

For the analysts and journalists, the professional track was a challenge. It gave them new ways to use their professional skills. But *Affärsvärlden*'s administrators, marketers, and salespeople were less keen on it. They regarded the analytical projects as trivial and the database investment as outrageously expensive, and they were no more sanguine about consulting services. Consulting services demand knowledge-focused strategies, and none of the salespeople were qualified to sell them. In contrast, these people were interested in the organizational track.

THE ORGANIZATIONAL TRACK

Around 1981, the *Affärsvärlden* management began formulating a strategy for developing the group's magazines. The idea was to concentrate on three areas: finance and the stock market, management, and small business. The basic rationale was that there was much to be gained from coordinating marketing and advertising sales visits, for example, and running joint supplements and campaigns. The administrators loved the idea because it would spread out the costs of subscription management, invoicing, and booking systems. It gave the administrators and salespeople a bigger canvas to work with in areas they knew about, as well as more titles to sell advertising space in. It seemed a natural way to expand the business.

So *Affärsvärlden* launched a management magazine, *Ledarskap* (*Leadership*), a management magazine for small businesses, *Affärer och Företag* (*Business and Companies*), and various newsletters. The *Affärsvärlden* partners, who were primarily journalists and financial analysts, were not particularly interested in this publishing route because the concerns of small grocery proprietors, for example, seemed trivial compared with the dramatic movements in the capital market and the activities of multinationals such as Ericsson and of big-time operators like Jan Carlzon of SAS and P. G. Gyllenhammar of Volvo.

Journals compete in the information market, and the Swedish press suffers from the same overcapacity as its counterparts in other developed countries. Barely one in one hundred new launches succeeds, but those that manage to find new advertising niches can make lots of money. Information products are easy to copy, so new launches in the financial, business, and management segments came thick and fast during the 1980s. *Ledarskap* survived for nine years and can thus be deemed a moderate success. The newsletters also did quite well, but the small business magazine folded after two years.

THE STRATEGIC DILEMMA

In newspaper and magazine publishing firms, as in most other companies, strategy is normally management's responsibility, which is to say it is determined by the managers rather than the professionals. The normal direction of expansion in publishing is thus organizational. And managers naturally prefer to go for projects that present new challenges to their own management skills, which, in the publishing business, means adding magazines or other titles, as in *Affärsvärlden*'s organizational track.

The company Affärsvärlden is unusual in that it also developed along the other axis—still within the scope of its editorial core competencies but into new areas of management, which I have called the professional track. These new ventures were successful in business terms but developed so strongly that they diverged from *Affärsvärlden*'s mainstream strategy.

Instead of either forcing the new businesses to accept the group's mainstream strategy or adapting the strategy to suit the new businesses, the partners chose to sell the subsidiaries and let them develop independently. In the end the analytical projects succeeded, partly because the market for financial analysis skills was buoyant and partly because they successfully pursued knowledge-focused strategies. They were launched by financial analysts who also possessed a talent for organization. The organizational track fared less well, partly because there was already a glut in information markets and partly because at least one of the projects was launched without its own journalistic competence.

LESSONS TO BE LEARNED

This case study makes it clear that one must beware when entering information markets if one intends to rely on revenues from readers or consumers of information. They tend to be overcatered to and unwilling to pay. In addition, unlike in the manufacturing industry where the managers are in control, a choice of strategy in a knowledge organization has more to do with which tradition of knowledge is in control. Experts are likely to choose a professional route; managers are more inclined to go the organizational way.

A company needs both knowledge traditions to be successful. Professionals are likely to disregard the long-term management problems of their preferred expansion route, and managers will have problems in managing the professionals. Whatever strategic choice one makes, one is likely to alienate one of the two main groups contending for power—the managers or the professionals. This is one of the critical dilemmas of the knowledge organization.

As venture capitalists know, the reins of new knowledge business ventures should be held by people who are familiar with their intellectual content, probably the experts. The managers should play second fiddle during the first few years of a project.

⁗ The Industrial Age Paradigm and the Information-Focused Strategy

Information-focused strategies maintain many of the attributes of an industrial age perspective on business. The industrial age perspective still guides business strategy, particularly in old, large companies founded during the height of the industrial age (from the 1800s until World War II). From an industrial age perspective, information technology is just like any other technology, albeit very versatile.

There is much to be said for the industrial age perspective. First, it is efficient because output per person increases when computers are substituted for people. This has been the rationale for new technology since the dawn of the factory age, and it remains just as valid today. Even in areas relatively untouched by information technology, industrial methods often offer a major competitive advantage. The fast food industry, for example, is a blueprint of a Tayloristic assembly line principle that includes the customer to minimize the time it takes to fill an empty stomach. Second, the goods and services produced by companies pursuing industrial age strategies are readily quantifiable. Managers can rely on the financial accounts. Customers can perceive a tangible value in a plateful of food delivered within three minutes, a management book comprising a thousand pages at a cost of one cent per page, or a very long journey that costs little per mile. Third, it offers consistency and predictability. Big Macs or Mars Bars taste more or less the same everywhere; a copy of a computer program is identical to the original. There are no surprises, whether pleasant or unpleasant. Finally, this strategy offers control. When information technology is substituted for people, the process seems more manageable because it is easier to control computers than people. And it is no trouble at all for computers to control other computers. Division of labor and systematic measurement also make it easier to control the people who are needed.

So manufacturing companies make the most use of IT by molding their strategies to be more information-focused; they put computer chips in their products and develop cars that diagnose themselves and warn drivers of everything from a flat tire (Goodyear's Smart Tires) to the fact that they have taken a wrong turn (Radio Data System and satellite surveillance). These days, even windows are smart enough—if they're coated with Cloud Gel—to adjust the heat radiation they let in to the inside temperature. Service companies use information for communications and for learning more about their customers. There are elevators that automatically alert maintenance engineers to incipient faults (Otis) and hotels that compile customer profiles in their computer systems so that they can render customized personal service (Ritz–Carlton). Knowledge organizations like Netscape and Microsoft use IT to sell the competence of their experts as software packages and for communication. Financial information firms like Extel supply data and analytical software on diskettes or on–line.

The industrial age perspective is common in both manufacturing and service industries, and is generally regarded as common sense and even inevitable. Sociologists (Ritzer 1993) call it the "McDonaldization" process and bemoan it as a natural development inspired by man's desire—noted as early as 1905 by Max Weber in *The Protestant Ethic and the Spirit of Capitalism* (1986)—to rationalize his environment.

An information–focused strategy looks indeed like the old industrialization process dressed up in silicon. But can McDonaldization propose a winning strategy for the knowledge era?

WHAT'S WRONG WITH THE INFORMATION FOCUS?

Information technology can be used to standardize or to customize. It can be used to increase control over people or to decrease it. It can be used to control very large bureaucracies or empower very large networks. It can be a powerful servant of an industrial strategy, an information–focused strategy, or a powerful enabler of a knowledge–focused strategy. The choice is made not by the technology but by those in power. And they make their decisions guided by their perspective.

The most serious problem with strategies guided by an industrial age paradigm is that, as the Saatchis discovered, they tend to underuse intangible assets and provoke fierce internal conflicts that can gravely damage the company's development, profitability, or both. The other critical problem with an information–focused strategy is the ease of copying it. It is impossible to achieve a long–term competitive advantage with IT because it is available to everyone. Those who embark on a strategy of IT leadership find that they must run faster and faster just to stay in place. Increasing returns are available only to the winner while the runners–up have a hard time. Microsoft, despite being one of the new breed of knowledge companies and the present leader in its industry, provides a cautionary tale in this respect.

Until now, Microsoft has pursued something that looks like an information–focused strategy, and the company is therefore exposed to the forces of the information markets. In response, the company is reducing the price of its software by bundling it into larger and larger packages of ever-cheaper "bloatware." The price per information bit is thus sinking rapidly. This has been widely regarded as a method to block competition, and it works fine for the leader. But Microsoft is as vulnerable as anybody else to the effects of an information-focused strategy: once you make your tacit knowledge explicit or informatize your offering, you open yourself up to copycats and are forced to reduce the price. The only alternative available is to run fast.

Microsoft created the PC software standard before the Internet and has been running faster than everybody else, until Netscape lunged onto the scene. It came close to missing the Internet boat. But the company culture, described sometimes as paranoid, might have saved it this time. Microsoft is now vigorously catching up lost terrain but is still lagging behind the new leader, Netscape. In 1996, Microsoft is still growing very fast and is very profitable, but its annual reports reveal little about the true state of its intangible assets—whether they are increasing or deteriorating—and very little about how the company manages them.

CAN A KNOWLEDGE-FOCUSED STRATEGY BE WISE MANAGEMENT?

If an information-based strategy has problems, can a knowledge-focused strategy replace it?

First, can it be efficient? It depends on what is meant by efficient. As the *Affärsvärlden*, McKinsey, and WM-data cases show, companies that opt for a knowledge-focused strategy can certainly be very profitable. (This issue is discussed at greater length in Chapter 13.) The issue is not about efficiency but about effectiveness. Knowledge strategies focus on the potential of professionals to increase revenue rather than on the ability of managers to reduce costs, and they define *revenue* broadly—to include all the good things that come from their customers, including methodology, experience, and image, as well as money.

Can a knowledge-focused strategy be quantifiable? Certainly, if ways can be found to measure not only the flows of money but also the flows affecting the intangible assets. Movement in a company's intangible assets is the underlying cause of much unexpected movement in revenues and costs.

Is a knowledge-focused strategy controllable? Yes. As WM-data proves, a large firm can run a very tightly controlled operation by designing a management information system that monitors the intangible assets. Companies like McKinsey and *Affärsvärlden* control their operations with strong cultures.

Can a knowledge–focused strategy be copied? No. Initiation is difficult and takes time because the strategy is embedded in relationships with customers and people. This may explain why some niche players are so competitive in knowledge markets despite their lack of a superior competence or technology. Their niche consists of a particular person's expertise or the relationships with particular customers he or she nurtures.

Can the knowledge–focused strategy be predictable? Yes, but this is one of its perceived weaknesses today. Managers operating under an industrial age perspective probably feel that investments in knowledge–based assets are less predictable than investments in computer systems. Many customers also like assurance before they buy a solution, but if the product is created in a dialogue—as it is with a knowledge–focused strategy—customers will not know what they get until they've got it. This is a marketing dilemma shared by all services.

A knowledge–focused strategy can be very competitive not only because it utilizes the unlimited resources of knowledge but also because it goes against common sense in many industries, as the *Affärsvärlden* case illustrates. Strategies that break with "common sense" can catch competitors by surprise.

In fact, a knowledge–focused strategy is probably less risky than an information–focused strategy. Take, for example, the risky nature of the information markets I describe in Chapter 9. Or, consider that shares in software companies tend to be much more volatile than shares in business service companies. For example, software companies listed on the Sydney stock exchange in August 1996 had average beta values of 1.2 while business services averaged 0.55.[2] In other words, information–related companies were twice as volatile as knowledge–related firms at that time.

A knowledge–focused strategy can give new business opportunities because once–unidentified intangible assets now may prove to be a valuable source of tangible revenues. The insurance company Skandia, for example, has identified a number of administrative processes traditionally regarded as background processes and sold them to other insurance companies. Furthermore, a knowledge–focused strategy does not exclude information technology. It is true that most corporate IT systems bear the imprint of obsolete industrial paradigms, but that is not in the nature of the technology. IT is used to make the operation more efficient and to improve information transfer. The Internet, multimedia, and groupware, like Lotus Notes, are making it easier and easier to run very large operations with very loose information systems.

As yet there is no software that can transfer knowledge in a way that makes use of the human ability to learn with all senses. It is far harder and takes far longer to transfer competence from one person to another than to convey information. It is not yet possible to clone competence, although some progress has been made in this area by companies like Skandia AFS. Technology to embed expertise in artificial intelligence or expert systems is still in its infancy. Because it is being developed within an industrial paradigm, the likelihood is that when it comes of age, it will act, initially at any rate, as an agent of McDonaldization. So let us not be so blinded by the wizardry of computers that we forget that noncomputerized methods for knowledge transfer are still far more effective.

So what *is* wrong with a knowledge–focused strategy? Very little. The main problem for those wishing to adopt it is that the ghost of the industrial age still haunts the business environment. A strategy that defies common sense can be hard to sell. Those attracted to the knowledge route can't look to academic research for guidance because there is very little available. They can't look to consultants because most are information–focused. Consider the fate of business process reengineering (BPR), the "big idea" of management academics and consultants in the mid–1990s. BPR consultants promised huge rewards if companies exchanged their people for computerized processes. But by dispensing with people, firms were unwittingly eroding their knowledge base. Many sacrificed large numbers of people on the altar of BPR, only to find they had created chaos and alienated their most competent employees. Happily, BPR is now consigned to the dustbin for dead ideas, forced there by that industrial age ghost that still sees people as costs rather than revenues.

Can large companies use a knowledge–focused strategy? I do not believe creativity can flourish in large organizations because of the inevitable spread of bureaucracy. But one way for large firms to deal with this problem is to assemble small creative teams—pro–teams—within large units and use the energy that builds up between them and the main organization in constructive ways. That is what I call the pro–team organization, discussed in Chapter 8.

In the end it is not really a question of which strategy to choose but rather of how to live with both. Organizations need a little of both. They need efficiency and effectiveness, routine and renewal. The best course may be to supply *both* customized solutions and standardized packages. Can two such different strategies coexist in the same organization? The next section demonstrates that the answer is yes.

ꜙ Knowledge-Focused Strategies in Industry

The knowledge-focused strategy involves the selling of professional skills to solve problems and is of course the normal strategy for consultants and professional service companies. But it is in many ways the opposite of industrialization. Does it make sense in the manufacturing industry?

Selling solutions rather than products has been standard procedure in most industries for almost two decades now. The solutions involve both IT systems and people, and they are increasingly so sophisticated that the hardware part is negligible. Some even sell their organizational knowledge.

For example, to its customers around the world, Finnish special-metals group Outukumppu sells not only metal but also know-how in the form of ready-made smelting plants, complete with education for supervisory personnel. Air Products, the industrial gases group, sells not only cryogens (liquid gases) but also its knowledge about how to transport, store, and handle these hazardous substances.

IT allows manufacturing companies to manufacture ever-shorter runs and thus to customize their products. This eliminates traditional unskilled jobs, turning workers into IT professionals who monitor rather than operate computer-controlled machines or processes. Such developments are bringing the factory ever closer to customers. It would not be surprising if before long customers talk directly to the machine monitors.

Manufacturing firms will come to depend more and more on their few remaining skilled workers whose status will begin to approach that of a knowledge company's professionals. Moreover, the logic of the customization idea compels manufacturers to establish closer relations with their customers and thus to become even more involved in solving their problems rather than merely selling them products.

Signs that traditional industry is becoming increasingly intangible are not hard to find. But they are using the information-focused strategy to do so. Companies are packing their products and solutions with software and capturing organizational knowledge on computer software; this process will eventually expose them to the forces of informatized markets.

Is there a profitable way out of this rat race? Let us contemplate what a knowledge-focused strategy would mean for one of the United States' oldest manufacturing companies, Goulds Pumps.

▪' Goulds Pumps: From High-Tech to Commodity

Goulds Pumps is one of the oldest and best-known pump manufacturers in the world. Founded in 1848, the company developed early know-how in metal casting and used it to create various pieces of machinery, one of which was the world's first entirely metal water pump. The business grew steadily during the 1800s and early 1900s, with major growth spurts during both of the two world wars (again partially as a result of expertise in metals).

In the late 1950s and early 1960s, Goulds became increasingly innovative and developed highly successful chemical- and paper-making process pumps that incorporated a variety of technological design features that soon became de facto industry standards. These pumps were quite expensive, but they were considered the best available. However, although this design know-how had clearly given Goulds a competitive advantage, the products would have likely remained high-tech niche products had not the company shifted much of its energy into developing a strong marketing and sales organization. This organization, which came to be regarded as one of the strongest and most highly skilled in the industry, developed much of the company's know-how around customer processes and applications.

Like the early IBM, Goulds leveraged early technological innovation into a market-dominating advantage by shifting a know-how focus to customer applications and customized solutions to unique customer needs. It was a business strategy that generated strong sales and generous profits. Indeed, the company's stock grew and split so many times during the 1960s and 1970s that, as with the computer companies of the era, many people made a small fortune by investing in Goulds.

By the mid-1980s, however, the innovation rate dropped, the competitors caught up, and Goulds' customer base was moving toward increased standardization and cost containment. This also meant it was looking for more standardized pump solutions. A number of Goulds' competitors were quick to develop lower-cost alternatives that didn't have all the bells and whistles of Goulds' pumps but were adequate for the customer's needs. This created significant cost pressures for Goulds, which was not accustomed to viewing its product as a commodity. Nor had it approached manufacturing or sales in a commodity product fashion.

Goulds shifted strategy. For the last eight years the company has been pouring resources into IT in the form of processes and technology geared toward helping it become a successful producer of a commodity product in a commodity market. Similarly, it has shifted its sales focus toward offering standardized solution packages to their customers rather than offering the customized pumps of previous years. So, in the terminology of this book, where Goulds once had a knowledge (technology) focus it has shifted to an information focus. It has reduced its costs with computer systems, standardized its pumps to make them easier to manufacture and package for customers, used IT to reduce its workforce, and computerized its production and order-entry processes. It has moved some production to lower-cost countries. It has focused its factories and formed a centralized customer service organization to save administrative costs.

Goulds has been pretty good at its new strategy. Through cost cutting and substituting IT for personnel, it has maintained a return on equity of around 12 percent to 14 percent since 1991 on stagnant sales: in 1995, sales totaled $600 million, barely up from $557 million in 1994. But Goulds' competitors have been doing the same thing as Goulds has—many more quickly and effectively than Goulds—so its share price is lagging, as shown in Figure 19.

Figure 20 shows the company's stagnant book value. For Goulds this means that there is ever-increasing pressure on costs and lead time as its customers and competition continue to commoditize the product.

It is no good to be the runner-up in an informatized market, and the way the pump industry is going it will become increasingly informatized. Is Goulds trapped or can it break out of this commodity-based rat race? One strategy, of course, is to play the commodity game better than anyone else and try to be the cost leader. Keep on cutting costs, reengineering the processes, and trimming overhead costs (including the sales force), simplifying the product, and so on. But given its history, this may be a strategy ill-suited for a company like Goulds.

Share Price

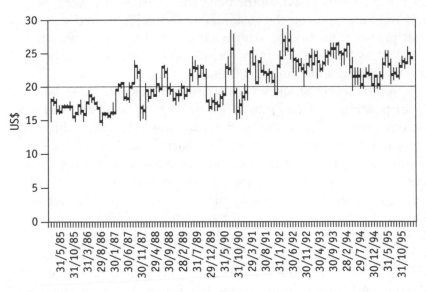

Figure 19. Goulds Pumps' strategy has not brought shareholder value in eight years.

Stock Market Value

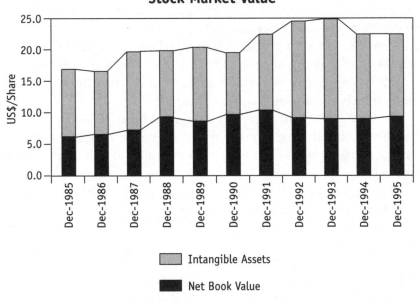

Figure 20. Goulds' net book value has been stagnant for eight years. The key to improvement may be found among its intangible assets.

THE ALTERNATIVE: A KNOWLEDGE-FOCUSED STRATEGY

As in any big company, there are pockets or divisions within the Goulds organization where the overall corporate strategy has not been implemented. One of those pockets is a small division on the West Coast that continues to produce tailor-made pumps for highly specialized applications. These pumps are produced in projectlike form, with the engineers acting as consultants to their customers. Similarly, the factory employees are highly skilled and flexible, much like the craft guilds of the turn of century. Yet the factory is under threat because its costs are higher and its lead times longer than elsewhere in Goulds. The tailor-made pumps offer higher margins but not sufficiently high to offset the higher costs.

Fortunately, a number of Goulds sales engineers are still capable of and appreciate the challenge of selling highly customized pump solutions. Unfortunately, they are not employed by the division itself but rather are part of a generalized sales organization that sells the entire portfolio of Goulds products. Understandably, the division's managers complain that the corporate salespeople do not allocate enough time for their products while the sales managers reply that the specialized pumps take too much time to sell compared with the volume and overall margin they yield.

The alternative is to pursue a knowledge-focused strategy by leveraging the division's three key intangible assets: the competence of its people, its external structure (customer and vendor relations), and its internal structure (management, IT systems, and R&D).

The West Coast division has large unmeasured and therefore probably underutilized intangible assets in its craftsmen and its image of producing high-quality pumps. To make full use of these intangible assets, it must focus on these assets and make them its prime concern. Learning how to do this may be the unique contribution of the small West Coast division. The division will have to deal with many issues.

ISSUES OF COMPETENCE

The division must see the craftsmen and the key salespeople as potential revenue creators, rather than cost items, and stop exchanging workers for IT. It will need to recruit new highly qualified production personnel. It must develop robust processes for transferring the skills of the most qualified workers to the new recruits and consider using the more experienced workers as coaches or mentors.

Because it is subject to the efforts of one large generalized sales force, it should focus on helping the sales engineers better understand what the division can do by aggressively educating them about the division's capabilities. Similarly, given the pumps' more customized applications, the division's managers must educate the salespeople to ensure that they can work with the division's more demanding customers.

ISSUES OF INTERNAL STRUCTURE

The division will have to invest in computer support systems for the workforce so it can react quickly to customer feedback. It may consider artificial intelligence systems that capitalize on some of the expertise held by the older workers.

It should try to take on large assignments that allow for use of teams and then create positions in the teams for juniors and seniors to work alongside one another. Professional careers for workers and engineers should be established, with the best of these employees remunerated as well as or better than managers.

R&D projects should be initiated to speed up manufacturing and customization processes. The division should develop and maintain some new nonfinancial ratios to make invisible assets more visible and to guide its new strategy.

EXTERNAL STRUCTURE, CUSTOMER, AND VENDOR ISSUES

The division should attempt to develop a much closer relationship with its customers in order to make full use of the intangible revenues. The salespeople are highly qualified engineers, which is a good start, but the division must gain control over its own customer relations by allowing its craftsmen to come closer to the customers, either by promoting some of them to sales engineers or by taking over some of the parent company's sales force. Furthermore, the sales staff needs to come closer to the factory and the actual production. It will also be important to find ways to get production closer to the customers.

The customers who are the more profitable, have the highest image, and bring learning and know-how to division employees should be identified and ways to improve relations with them determined. Also, potential customers who have the "sexiest," that is, most difficult pump issues, should be identified and sought after. In addition, existing "good chemistry" and the customers with which it has had long–lasting relationships should be identified. What more can be done for them? Can Goulds offer service and maintain complex processes for them rather than just pumps?

Ways that vendors can contribute competence to the workforce and to the sales force should be identified, knowledge–sharing partnerships with suppliers developed. The division should seek to learn from every supplier interaction. The division should develop a high-quality, flexible, and competent supplier base. It should invest in processes and systems that enable quick and effective integration of customized supplier solutions into unique customer solutions. It should create IT systems for sharing information about the implementation of larger projects. Workers, engineers, and salesmen should contribute information. Finally, the division should determine whether Goulds can create standards for its customers' knowledge creation, such as a data bank with benchmark data from installations all over the world so that customers can compare its service with others.

These actions are not easy to implement. They are also quite different from those that would be taken by a division seeking an industrial–model, low–cost commodity–based solution. Through these actions, this company would seek to rediscover the leverage of knowledge. For this small division on the West Coast, these may be the strategies that enable it to survive and prosper.

Summary

■ A knowledge–focused strategy may be applicable for a wide range of industries and organizations because every organization has competent people, an internal structure that can be made more efficient, and an external structure the management of which can produce visible and invisible revenues from customers.

■ In the manufacturing industry managers are in power. But in a knowledge organization, the business strategy is a question of which tradition of knowledge is in control. Experts are likely to choose a professional route; managers the organizational route.

■ Information–focused strategies have many of the attributes of an industrial age perspective on doing business. They tend to under-use intangible assets and are easy to copy.

■ Knowledge–focused strategies are effective rather than efficient; they can be quantified and controlled; they are difficult to copy and thus less risky. They can be used by all kinds of industries, including manufacturing. The latter firms are becoming more like knowledge companies as their few remaining workers become as valuable as professionals and as the companies themselves are more likely to sell solutions than products.

Advice to Managers

- New knowledge businesses should be founded with both organizational and professional knowledge available. The professionals should have the strategic initiative during the early period.

3
Measuring Intangible Assets

Measuring Intangible Assets

The chapters in this last section outline a nonfinancial measurement system for intangible assets based on the concept of the knowledge organization.

The measuring system that I propose does not present a full and comprehensive picture of a company's intangible assets; such a system is not possible. That is why the all-comprehensive approaches have failed so far. Rather, the purpose here is to be practical, to "open a few windows" so that managers can at least begin measuring their firms.

Chapter 11 provides a perspective by discussing the kinds of measurement activities that have been done to date. Chapter 12 outlines specific measures for each of the three types of intangible assets. Finally, Chapter 13 presents several case studies that show how leading companies in the area of measuring intangible assets do so.

The State of the Art of
Measuring Intangible Assets

This chapter offers a perspective on measuring intangible assets. It begins by discussing the measurement systems already devised for intangible assets and then presents a new framework for what I believe is a superior and workable system.

⁙ A Perspective on Measurement

Much of the international research on measuring intangible assets has used financial variables only; that is, employees are treated as balance sheet items that can be measured in dollars. Some theories introduce probabilities or discount a person's output during a lifetime in the traditional balance sheet. Although theoretically interesting, little of the attempts to convert people or competencies into dollars has proved useful for managers (Gröjer and Johansson 1991; Johansson and Nilson 1990b).

Research in human resource costing and accounting has brought forward some interesting Swedish projects, both at Ericsson and, in the public sector, at Swedish Telecom Telia, with an emphasis on personnel accounting calculations for use in decision making (Johansson and Nilson 1994; *Journal of HRCA* 1994, Vol. 1, No. 1). For instance, they have assessed the costs of sick leaves and personnel turnover and designed indicators that can be used as rules of thumb by managers.

When profits or cash flow are related to tangible assets, capital employed, or equity, the argument in the favor of such systems is that only by focusing on tangible flows are shareholders guaranteed that management will create shareholder value. They may remind the

CEO to keep shareholder interest in mind, but it is dangerous—as some enthusiastic supporters argue—to use such ratios for operational control.

These systems do not shed light on the whole range of intangible assets that exist, and they are not useful as management information systems monitoring the daily progress of a business. But as the case study of WM-data that appears later in this chapter shows, it is possible to create superior shareholder value by focusing not on the tangible but on the intangible assets.

The more ambitious proposals so far share another fundamental flaw: they tend to be based on an implicit manufacturing or industrial perspective. They do not take into account that service companies account for 65 percent to 75 percent of the employment in the industrialized world and that the rapidly growing, largely unresearched subsector that I call knowledge organizations is already bypassing the manufacturing sector in many countries.

◢ Investment in Intangible Assets

Depending on one's perspective any indicator is subject to a large number of possible interpretations, so the coherent conceptual framework is the fundament that must be built first. For example, let us consider the issue of what constitutes an investment.

When a company invests in material assets like machines or computers, the money is paid out of liquid funds and a corresponding amount is booked as an asset on the balance sheet under a heading—machinery, for example. In accounting terms, there has been a negative cash flow but no cost. The cost is incurred gradually as the asset is depreciated.

In contrast, when a company invests in an intangible asset, such as when it launches a research program or enters a new market segment, it is not generally permitted to record the value of the research as an asset on the balance sheet. The investment thus appears both as a negative cash flow and as a cost item.

Both types of investment are inspired by the same motive: to achieve higher profitability in the long term by sacrificing cash flow in the short term. The difference in accounting treatment, however, is very confusing and is made more so because the "cost" of intangible investments can take a form other than direct payment from cash reserves. It may take the form, for example, of accepting an assignment that yields little cash revenue but has great publicity value or seems likely to enhance competence. Here again the intangible asset is financed by "invisible" equity.

R&D generates value that is clearly owned by the company, so it is reasonable to regard such expenditures as an investment. True, the economic value is uncertain, but the same may be said of any investment, including the value of center-city office buildings, as many investors have learned the hard way in recent years. But cash outlay for knowledge acquisition is not always an intangible asset. Many commentators insist that training and education costs should be viewed as investments, but to whom or what does the value created by such investment adhere? When individuals pay for their own education, they are investing their own personal capital, but when such education is paid for by the company, the link between payer and asset is broken, and the company is paying for an asset that it will not own. Individual competence is "owned" by individuals and not by companies, so from the company's point of view money spent on educating employees should be treated as a cost rather than as an investment.[1]

⁙ Measuring Yield

The difficulty in using financial variables alone to measure knowledge companies' value can be seen by examining yield. Measurements of profit are interesting because they show how much is "left over" for the shareholders when everything and everybody else have been paid off. However, as every accountant worth his salt knows, there are so many ways to distort one year's profit figure that the truth is in the eye of the beholder.

R&D is sometimes treated as an investment, sometimes as a cost. If a company displays increased profit because of reduction in R&D, is that a real profit or not? Reported profits of privately held companies are customarily very small because the desire to demonstrate the organization's success is more than outweighed by the desire to avoid paying a penny more in company tax than is absolutely necessary. And how do you value work in progress? Hidden factors like invoicing being delayed or brought forward can heavily influence reported figures. Large effects on the reported profit figures are often due to unidentified changes in intangible assets. These multiply the problems even further.

Profits are simply not a good yardstick for comparing companies with large intangible assets. The least helpful profit indicators are return on equity or return on assets. More useful are profit margin measures like profit as a percent of sales or—best—profit as a percent of value added.

PROFIT MARGIN

Profit margin is a key indicator that describes the profit-generating capacity of the revenue flow. Profit margin is an important indicator of the attractiveness of investing money in a knowledge company, but it does not tell much about the actual efficiency of its employees. Nevertheless, profit margin is generally a better measure of efficiency than return on equity or investment, for example, which is totally irrelevant in companies where financial capital plays an insignificant part.

Profit margins vary a great deal from one industry to another. A better way of expressing profit margin is therefore to use the ratio of profit to value added.

EFFICIENCY AND EFFECTIVENESS

As discussed in Chapter 8, efficiency and effectiveness are two different indicators. Efficiency is calculated solely on input variables; effectiveness is calculated with both input and output variables. Efficiency measures show how well an organization is using its capacity regardless of what it produces. A criterion of efficiency often used by consulting firms is billable time, that is, time billed to clients as a proportion of time available. This measures how much time consultants are paid for. It is a simple and good indicator of short-term profitability because it measures capacity usage, but it says nothing about what the consultants accomplish in that time.

Effectiveness measures show how well an organization is satisfying the needs of those it serves. The needs of the various parties concerned may, of course, differ: shareholders are interested in dividends while customers are interested in service levels and quality. Firms should, therefore, employ different efficiency measures for different audiences.

ROI (return on invested capital) is a criterion of efficiency popular in financial circles. It measures profit generated by the capital invested in a company or a project and is thus a very important indicator of the efficiency of the capital invested, both to creditors and to owners of the invested capital. For shareholders, the most important figure is what they earn after tax in the form of dividends on the capital they have put into the company, that is, the return after tax on their own equity, often shortened to ROE.

Management must also track the return on the firm's total capital and on particular investment projects so that it can control the allocation of capital. Unfortunately, this technique cannot be applied to intangible assets, so various income statements and nonfinancial measurements must be used instead to calculate efficiency.

Effectiveness is also difficult to measure because one must often go outside one's own organization. To measure customer satisfaction—an important indicator for effectiveness—one must rely on customer polls. Therefore, effectiveness is seldom measured.

Even if it is not possible to measure effectiveness, it is nevertheless valuable to think in effectiveness terms. What gives the most revealing picture of performance: focusing on the costs of people or on the revenues they bring in? Cost focus is efficiency-oriented, revenue focus is effectiveness-oriented.

The solution is in measuring *value added,* a term frequently used by economists but sadly neglected in the field of corporate financial analysis. In brief, value added is the increase in value that employees (or professionals) create after deducting all purchases from external sources. (Value added and how to calculate it will be discussed in more depth in Chapter 12.) It exemplifies the correct measure for the production ability of a knowledge company and the shortfall of traditional financial measures.

." Why Nonfinancial Measures?

It is tempting to try to design a measurement-system equivalent to double-entry bookkeeping with money as the common denominator. It is an established framework with definitions and standards and therefore common sense. But this is precisely the reason why we should break with it.

If we measure the new with the tools of the old, we won't be able to perceive the new. Any measurement system is limited by Heisenberg's uncertainty principle, according to which it is impossible to measure simultaneously the speed and the position of particles. The physicist Bohr (with whom Einstein disagreed) argued that this means that the observer is always involved in the measurement and that the physical world does not have well-defined attributes.

If truth is in the eye of the beholder in the physical world, it is even more so in the world of business. There is no difference between financial measures and other measures. Both are uncertain; all depend on the observer. There exist no objective measures. The main reasons why financial measures seem more objective or "real" are that they are founded on implicit concepts of what a company is and have been around for so long that they are guided by definitions and standards.

Once measures have been selected, they color what we see and how we act. The problem with translating actions into money is that very few people in an organization handle money directly. Most of them work by using their competencies in the service of customers. Money is merely a proxy for human effort, and the five-hundred-year-old system of accounting sheds little light on the vital processes in organizations whose assets are largely nonfinancial and intangible.

Still, there exists no comprehensive system for measuring intangible assets that uses money as the common denominator and at the same time is practical and useful for managers. Depending on the purpose for measuring, I do not think such a system is necessary, either. Knowledge flows and intangible assets are essentially nonfinancial. We need new proxies.

Nonfinancial information systems might become more popular in the manufacturing industry too. Kaplan and Norton (1996) suggest a "balanced scorecard" that complements the traditional financial perspective with three nonfinancial focuses: customers, internal processes, and innovation/improvement. Even though they discuss the subject from a manufacturing perspective, they argue for the use of nonfinancial measures. The process they suggest for identifying and computing indicators is compatible with the one I suggest in this book.

The lack of a coherent theoretical framework that fits the emerging knowledge industries is characteristic of the present development: it is not the academic world that has been defining the turf so far. Instead it seems that an emerging practice is currently driving the concept makers.[2]

Most companies measure at least some of their intangible assets and use nonfinancial indicators particularly for measuring operational efficiency. Manufacturing companies have, for instance, measured their output in tons per hour, hospitals and hotels measure bed utilization, schools measure average marks, universities measure number of Ph.D. dissertations per year, and so on. Operational efficiency—the efficiency of the internal structure—has been measured at least since the birth of the industrial organization. The other two intangible assets have begun to be measured much more recently: external structures, such as customer relations, are measured in the form of satisfaction levels, and competence is measured in the form of employee satisfaction and retention. But neither is monitored on a regular basis by most companies as yet.

The problem is not that intangible measures are difficult to design. Rather, the outcomes seem difficult to interpret. When used systematically, customer surveys yield an abundance of data that managers find difficult to correlate with changes in business performance. Kodak, for instance, does a monthly survey of some three hundred customers in each area of the business, asking specific open-ended questions. As a Kodak manager says, "The answer is almost impossible. We know we are often measuring dissatisfiers rather than satisfiers."[3]

This manager airs most managers' frustration with the lack of correct and certain measures. Like most managers, he believes that financial measures are more "real" than other data and he has no framework to interpret his data. His framework must be replaced by a new one, one that fits today's reality with some kind of knowledge perspective.

Measuring in a general sense involves trying to identify the flows that change or otherwise influence the market value of assets, as shown in Exhibit 8. If we disregard the ordinary visible balance sheet, we are left with three quantities to measure: external structure, internal structure, and competence of personnel.

Visible Equity	Intangible Assets		
Tangible assets minus visible liabilities	External structure	Internal structure	Competence of personnel

Exhibit 8. The market value of a company consists of its visible equity and intangible assets.

But can a management information system that uses both non-financial and financial measures guarantee financial success and shareholder value? Yes. Let us see how one of Europe's most profitable computer software and consulting companies, WM–data, monitors its knowledge–based strategy.

˒ WM-Data: Monitoring Intangible Assets for Financial Success

After a decade of unprecedented growth, WM–data is today the biggest of the publicly owned Swedish independent computer software and consulting companies. The main reason for its success is a very deliberate strategic policy that focuses on building corporate knowledge and customer relations and developing competence. In other words, WM–data has pursued a knowledge-focused strategy ever since its founding more than twenty–five years ago.

WM–data attributes its rapid growth to its lack of central head-quarter functions like marketing and human resources. The company consists of a web of quite independent subsidiaries and a small top management team. The corporate structure supports creativity and enables close customer relations. The ideal size of each work unit does not exceed fifty employees.

Top management keeps tight control with the support of a management information system. WM–data considers financial measures useless for management control and has designed a system of non-financial indicators that top management uses to follow operations on a weekly, monthly, and annual basis. WM–data uses traditional indicators like return on equity and return on investment only at the group level. Although WM–data does not use traditional financial indicators to control operations, there is nothing wrong with its financial performance. On the contrary, as Table 1 shows, it is one of the most profitable computer consulting firms in Europe.

As Figure 21 shows, the market value includes substantial intangible assets.

The core control element in WM–data's information system is the *revenue creating person* (RCP). The notion corresponds to that of the

	1985	1995	Average Increase 1985–95
Number of employees	273	3,040	+27.0%
Turnover (MSEK)	148	3,260	+36.0%
Net profit (MSEK)	31	316	+26.0%
Market value (MSEK)	155	4,300	+39.0%
	1991	**1995**	
Return on capital employed	38.5%	39.5%	
Return on equity	37.8%	32.7%	

Source: Company annual report, 1995.
Note: MSEK means millions of Swedish kronor.

Table 1. WM-data's financial performance, 1985 to 1995.

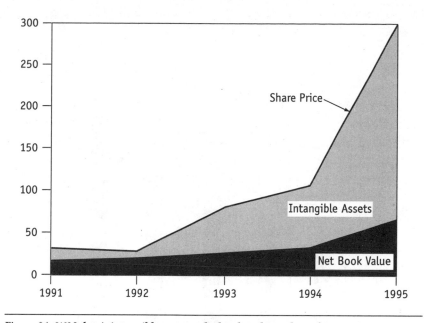

Figure 21. WM-data's intangible assets, calculated as the stock market premium over net book value per share. Source: Company annual report, 1995.

professional that I use in this book. The proportion of non–RCPs must never exceed 10 percent, as illustrated in Figure 22.

Another target statistic is personnel turnover, which WM–data endeavors to keep within a band of 7 percent to 10 percent. WM–data's operations require some turnover, but it must not be too quick. Although the company has to make a strenuous effort to keep personnel turnover below 10 percent in boom years, during the 1990 to 1993 recession in Sweden it increased personnel turnover by encouraging internal job rotation. Considerable resources are allocated to social activities to foster loyalty, for instance by engaging the families as members in the extended WM–data family. Figure 23 illustrates the results.

WM–data recruits actively from universities in order to prevent the corporate median age from creeping upward; the median age of all employees was thirty-four in 1995. A balance in age and experience is considered crucial in the fast-moving world of computer consulting.

For WM–data, a workforce balanced by gender is a strategic issue, not a nod to political correctness. The company wants to recruit more women because the company feels that doing so leads to a more creative atmosphere. But the company complains that young Swedish

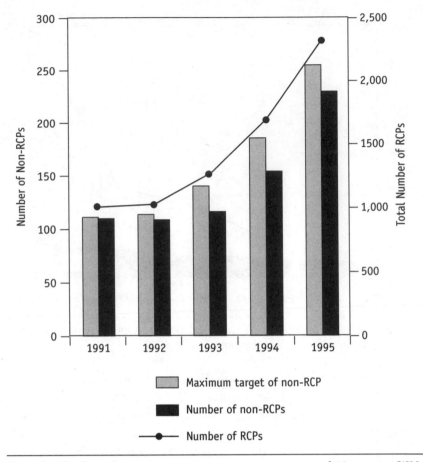

Figure 22. The share of nonrevenue creating persons may never exceed 10 percent at WM-data. Source: Company annual report, 1995.

women shun the computer professions, so the percentage of female employees is down to 29 percent.

At WM–data, weekly capacity utilization is the superior short–term profit thermometer; management knows that a one–hour decrease or increase in the number of hours billed during a week for the group as a whole translates into a sixty million Swedish kronor (MSEK) effect on the bottom line. If the indicator drops more than 10 percentage points, managers know that WM–data is operating in the red. But if it increases 10 percentage points, WM–data doubles the profit, which makes it tempting to push capacity utilization upward. WM–data considers 80 percent capacity utilization over a three–year period a target and sets prices and recruitment targets accordingly.

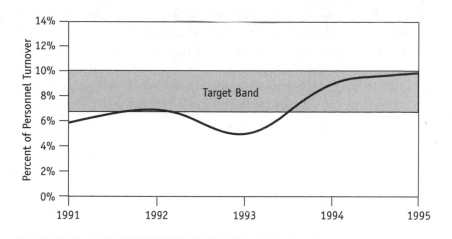

Figure 23. WM-data's personnel turnover is kept within a band of 7 percent to 10 percent. Source: Company annual report, 1995.

The founding tandem couple, Wilkne–Mellström, know that a higher utilization will burn out their experts—that is, their key professionals—many of whom have to work at 100 percent capacity to pull the average to an 80 percent rate. The 80 percent target gives flexibility in handling peak years and life–cycle plateaus.

Efficiency in the subsidiaries is measured as profit per RCP (up from TSEK—thousands of Swedish kronor—101 to TSEK 137 in 1995 and value added per RCP—increased by a fraction of a percent to TSEK 648 in 1995). Table 1 offers a glimpse of WM–data's 1995 annual report (see again Table 1).

LESSONS TO BE LEARNED

WM–data pursues a knowledge-focused strategy that includes many of the elements proposed in this book. Managers manage the environment or the spirit of the firm rather than supervise, and top management checks this environment with nonfinancial indicators. WM–data teaches us how to achieve financial success by focusing on intangible assets and monitoring indicators for them instead of traditional financial indicators.

Summary

- To date, systems for measuring intangible assets have been flawed by the use of financial variables with their industrial age perspective.

▪ Knowledge flows and intangible assets are nonfinancial and require both nonfinancial and financial measures.

▪ Interpreting nonfinancial measures has been a major stumbling block to their use. Such a framework now exists in the form of a knowledge perspective with the use of employee competence, internal structure, and external structure measurements.

12

Measuring Competence, Internal Structure, and External Structure

This chapter describes measurements for employee competence, internal structure, and external structure. The focus of the indicators presented in this chapter is to provide management control.

Before measurements may be taken, two preliminary steps are necessary: establishing the purpose of the measurements (that is, determining who will be interested in the results) and classifying the various employee groups under one of the three categories of intangible assets.

It should be noted that the indicators presented in this and the following chapter are suggestions and examples that must be adjusted to suit each company. They are not useful for all companies or under all circumstances.

◦▪ Determining the Purpose of the Measurement

There are two main purposes for measuring intangible assets and two main parties who will be interested in the results.

In the *external presentation*, the company describes itself as accurately as possible to stakeholders, customers, creditors, and shareholders so they can assess the quality of its management and whether it is likely to be a reliable supplier or a dependable creditor.

Internal measurement is undertaken for management, which needs to know as much as possible about the company so that it can monitor its progress and take corrective action when needed. That is, it provides a management information system.

The measurement's purpose raises another question. Should its focus be on levels or trends? In other words, should the value of intangible assets at a particular time be measured or should the attempt be to get a feel for changes and flows? Because business today is in a constant state of flux, it seems reasonable to conclude that managers are interested in flow and trends and that they are more concerned with the speed with which intangible assets are measured than with accuracy. This is an argument against converting the flows into monetary terms.

In contrast, external parties, although also interested in flow, are usually primarily interested in position because external accounts appear only at relatively lengthy intervals. Moreover, they wish to assess risk—that their loans will not be repaid or their equity will fall in value, for example. The presentation's form is also important to them, because they know less than the managers about how the business works.

Thus, the measurement's emphasis should be adapted to the end user. Management information should emphasize flow, change, and control figures, while external presentations should include key indicators and explanatory text because it is not possible to compile a full balance sheet that expresses in monetary terms every intangible asset.

As in all measurement systems, it is the comparisons that are interesting. A measurement tells nothing at all unless it is compared against a yardstick of some kind: another company, a previous year, or a budget, for example. When we measure intangible assets we must therefore be prepared to keep doing so for at least three measurement cycles before attempting to evaluate the results. Ideally, measurements should be repeated yearly.

Since we are redefining what is to be measured, we must also identify and remunerate the new contributors of data. When companies collect data with assistance from outside parties, they must be prepared to pay for this assistance, otherwise those involved—customers and suppliers—will be annoyed by all the surveys they have to fill in.

Exhibit 9 outlines the measurement indicators for the three intangible assets. They are *growth and renewal*—in other words, change—*efficiency*, and *stability*. Managers use all three of these measurement groups for internal purposes.

Management should select one or two indicators for each subheading in the exhibit. Computing more than one or two indicators for each subheading can be confusing to the reader. Displaying them

Competence	Internal Structure	External Structure
Indicators of Growth/Renewal	Indicators of Growth/Renewal	Indicators of Growth/Renewal
Indicators of Efficiency	Indicators of Efficiency	Indicators of Efficiency
Indicators of Stability	Indicators of Stability	Indicators of Stability

Exhibit 9. Indicators of intangible assets.

by way of a model that I call the Intangible Assets Monitor is then helpful. (An example of how a completed version of the model might look for a company is presented in Chapter 13.)

▪ Determining Whom to Measure

CLASSIFICATION BY CATEGORY OF EMPLOYEE

The next step is to classify all employee groups within one of two categories: professional or support staff.

Competence refers to the professionals' competence. As already discussed in the earlier chapters of this book, the term *professional* refers to the people who plan, produce, process, or present the products or solutions. These people are all directly involved in client work although they may or may not be professionals in the field of competence that constitutes the company's business idea.

So, should the financial controller be considered a professional? As discussed in Chapter 5, the answer is yes in reference to the financial field. But in many organizations the work of the financial controller is largely to preserve, maintain, and develop the internal rather than the external structure. This work is absolutely essential to the long-term viability of the organization, but it does not directly involve customers. Thus, this group of employees contributes to the internal structure.

The professional group also does not include members of the company's support staff, that is, those who work in accounting, administration, reception, and so on. The latter too contribute to the internal structure and should be measured under that category.

Outside experts and suppliers are also involved in projects. These independent contractors are an essential production factor in many companies. However, because they are not on the payroll, they should not be counted among the employees. The distinction between salaried and freelance personnel is in some ways arbitrary, but it is consistent with labor laws and statistics in most countries, so making this distinction makes comparisons easier.

Nevertheless, independent contractors are an important element in the external networks that a knowledge company builds to support the process of knowledge conversion. They should be considered under the external structure. The importance of independent contractors may become so great that the organization becomes virtual; that is, it ceases to be possible to see where the competence of the organization ends and that of its suppliers begins.

The problem of the gray areas—where employees perform a variety of duties—can be solved by including only the part of their time that is spent working for clients as professionals, with the rest charged to the internal structure. Time is such an important variable in knowledge organizations that it must be recorded.

CLASSIFICATION OF PROFESSIONAL COMPETENCE BY DEGREE OF RESPONSIBILITY

Many nonmanufacturing companies, especially knowledge companies, have a hierarchy depending on the degree of responsibility for customers. In an advertising company, for example, three levels may be distinguished:

- People who work on only part of a project
- Those with overall responsibility for a project (often called project managers)
- Those with overall responsibility for a given customer (often called account managers)

This kind of company often strives to develop and retain as many people as possible with overall customer responsibility because they are the key people.

Skills other than those of experts may be important enough to track, including, for example, the work of those whom I refer to as the *finders, minders,* and *grinders.* The finders are the people who are good at making contacts and bringing in new customers; the minders are the senior consultants; and the grinders are the unfortunate juniors who do all the hard work.

The Danish consultancy firm PLS–Consult classifies its staff in this manner. (PLS–Consult is discussed further later in this chapter.) The firm has what it calls *generators,* customer managers who are able to generate new customers; *leaders*, who manage major projects; and *teachers*, who pass their competence to others.

CLASSIFICATION OF PROFESSIONAL COMPETENCE BY AREA

Professional competence can also be divided among a company's divisions. An engineering consultancy, for example, might divide its competence between the power sector, physical communications, industrial construction, residential construction, and so on. A software consultancy might set its categories according to the number of professionals familiar with the different types of systems. The classification can be presented in diagrams. Again, the focus should be on comparison. Is the company gaining or losing competence in its core areas?

AN EXAMPLE OF THE USE OF CLASSIFICATION

The value in categorizing people is that the numbers can then be used as denominators to create indicators based on people rather than on financial capital. Several of the generic indicators in the Intangible Assets Monitor are based on such categorizations.

Jacobsen & Widmark is a Swedish technical engineering company that had nineteen hundred employees in 1995, sales of 1.2 billion Swedish kronor, and a profit of 84 million Swedish kronor before tax. It classifies its employees as follows:

Technicians	50
Consultants	900
Project leaders	650
Line managers	100
Support staff	200
Total	1,900

Based on such data, customized indicators can be calculated. For example, the Jacobsen & Widmark classifications can be used to make several important calculations:

Ratio of support staff to professionals:
$200/1,900 = 10.5$ percent

Sales per professional (all employees but support staff):
$1,218/1,700 = 716,740$ kronor

Sales per support staff: $1,218/200 = 6,090,000$ kronor
Project leaders, percent of professionals:
$650/1,700 = 38.2$ percent
Profit per professional: $84/1,700 = 49,411$ kronor

Whether ratios like these indicate good or poor performance or better or worse performance can only be determined when they are compared with previous years and with other industries.

The following sections describe how to use the measurements for growth and renewal, efficiency, and stability, first for competence and then for the internal and external structures.

,¹ Measuring Competence

Employee competence is not only one of the three intangible assets but also a source of the internal and external structures. As mentioned in the previous section, the competence discussed here refers to the competence of professionals.

GROWTH/RENEWAL

NUMBER OF YEARS IN THE PROFESSION

A simple and useful measure of competence is the total number of years that the company's professionals have worked in their profession. Although man–years per individual cannot, strictly speaking, be added, discrepancies are smoothed out enough over a group to make changes in the figure worth recording.

The total number of years in the profession is a measure of the skill and experience of a company's professional body, whereas professional experience per professional is a measure of the average skill and experience of each individual. The figure for competence per professional can be displayed on a graph with three to five classifications. The change in the indicator between two years shows how much the average competence is changing, which is a measure of growth or the renewal rate. The best way of presenting this is in a chart covering several years, but a table will do as well. (This will be illustrated by Table 6 in Chapter 13.)

LEVEL OF EDUCATION

The educational level of the professionals employed affects the assessment of their competence and thus the knowledge company's ability to achieve future success. Formal education is a valid indicator because students at academic levels learn to process vast amounts of information. There are three general educational classifications: primary, secondary, and tertiary. In organizations relying on a particular profession, like auditors, it is useful to distinguish how many are CPAs.

Average years of education can also be calculated. The change in the average indicates whether the company is improving its average educational level. (Again, see Table 6 in Chapter 13.)

It is interesting to keep a historical record of this information, both for internal use and for purposes of comparison with other companies in the same field of knowledge.

TRAINING AND EDUCATION COSTS

In knowledge companies, which depend so heavily on the knowledge and competence of their employees, competence development ought to be an item in which the company invests heavily, and it usually is. But this fact is not normally apparent from the company's financial statements because most knowledge is acquired not in formal courses but through regular assignments for customers and R&D projects.

Although the visible cost of training is not always high, it is still worth recording. Indicators measuring this include training costs as a percentage of turnover or the number of days devoted to education per professional. Training costs must of course also include the amount of time spent because time is generally the most expensive item.

GRADING

Generally speaking, educational level describes competence imprecisely. A better way is to award grades. Many companies, especially large multinationals, now grade their executives, but it is unusual to grade other employees. Yet grading professionals should not be difficult if career development discussions have already been introduced. A five-point or a three-point scale may be used. After grades are given, they can be analyzed with statistical methods. Then it is easy to trace how competence develops in various fields, how it changes with time, how it affects personnel turnover, and so on.

TURNOVER

If the competence of professionals who have joined the company is divided by the competence of those who have left it, the quotient shows how personnel turnover affects the company's competence.

Table 2 calculates competence turnover for a company with fifteen hundred employees. The change in years of experience is divided into three components: how much has been gained by new expansion recruitment (as opposed to merely adding one year to everybody), how much has been lost by departures, and how much has been gained or lost by replacing people who have left.

Competence Turnover, 1995	Years	Percent of Total
Years of experience gained by recruitment	150	1%
Years of experience lost with leavers	-132	1%
Years of experience gained with replacements	330	2%
Net increase in competence	348	2%

Note: Percentages derived by dividing numbers of years by 1,500, the total number of employees.

Table 2. Competence turnover.

COMPETENCE-ENHANCING CUSTOMERS

Because professionals spend most of their time working for customers and because customers are the most important source of competence development, valuable information can be gained by measuring the proportion of customer assignments that contribute to such a development. It is usually surprisingly easy to compile such information if employees are asked to identify the projects they consider to be educational, that is, R&D projects and so on. The PLS-Consult example later in this chapter and the Celemi example in Chapter 13 illustrate this indicator.

EFFICIENCY

PROPORTION OF PROFESSIONALS IN THE COMPANY

A key indicator of efficiency is the proportion of professionals in the firm, that is, the number of professionals divided by the total number of employees. This is a measure of how important the professionals are to the firm. This measure is useful in making comparisons between companies in the same business provided that the number of professionals is calculated in the same way for all the companies compared. It should be noted that the proportion of professionals varies from one business type to another and thus can be used only for comparisons within the same area of operations. See again, for example, the chart for WM-data in Figure 22, Chapter 11.

THE LEVERAGE EFFECT

The previous measurement also enables calculation of the *leverage effect* of the professionals. That is, how important are a company's in-house professionals to its ability to generate revenue? The formula is shown in Table 3.

This formula takes into account all the people engaged on projects, whether on salary or not. Doing this identifies the amount of earning power that is attributable to a firm's own professionals. The

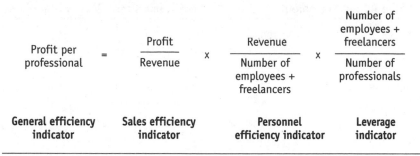

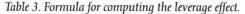

| General efficiency indicator | Sales efficiency indicator | Personnel efficiency indicator | Leverage indicator |

Table 3. Formula for computing the leverage effect.

leverage effect can be calculated at all levels and for all categories of people.

VALUE ADDED PER PROFESSIONAL

Value added per professional expresses how much value a company's professionals produce. As discussed in Chapter 11, value added is the best measure of yield. In knowledge companies, value added per professional can be regarded as the purest measure of ability to produce economic value. It is the professionals, by definition, who bring in all the revenue. These revenues must cover all the costs incurred in keeping the professionals in the field (that is, their travel, office, secretary, management, and administrative staff), as well as their own salaries, pensions, and so on. Much of the rest goes to finance equipment and its depreciation as well as to maintain knowledge capital, that is, training. The residual is the profit to be distributed as dividends to shareholders or used by the company for consolidation or investment. Table 4 illustrates how to do this for a nonmanufacturing company.

Value added per professional can also be calculated backwards, that is, by adding the profit before depreciation and interest to the sum of salaries, wages, and employers' social security contributions. The calculation involves adding operating profit of 21 to interest of 5 and salaries and so on of 65, for a total of 91. Fringe benefits, such as company cars, telephones, and so on, should also be included; simply include everything shown on pay slips.

The profit–generating ability of professionals depends on the state of the market, the efficiency of a company's management, and the amount of value added paid out directly to employees as salaries and benefits. For many knowledge organizations, the state of the market for their customers' customers is a critical factor. For example,

Value Added Statement		Traditional Profit & Loss Statement	
Income	100	Income	100
Goods purchased from outside suppliers	-5	Goods purchased from outside suppliers	-5
Rental on premises	-3	Rental on premises	-3
Leases on equipment	-1	Leases on equipment	-1
Total value added	91	Pay and employer's social contributions	-65
		Other personnel emoluments (fringe benefits, cars, etc.)	-5
Applied to		**Operating profit**	21
Pay and employer's contributions	65	Depreciation	-10
Other personnel emoluments	-5	**Profit after depreciation**	11
Depreciation	-10	Net interest	-5
Net interest	-5	**Profit before tax**	6
Profit before tax	6		
Number of employees	70	Operating margin	21%
Number of professionals	60	Net profit margin	6%
Profit as percent of value added	7%	Profit per employee	0.09
Value added per professional	1.52	Profit per professional	0.10

Table 4. A value added calculation.

when the construction and housing markets decline, the profit (and value added) per architect in architectural firms declines too. In boom times, the reverse is true. Advertising agencies and software consultants, in contrast, maintain more stable levels of payment through market fluctuations.

Because the professionals' salaries are normally the largest single cost item in a knowledge company's budget, profits are influenced by salary policies. In partnerships, salaries of the partners are often used as profit regulators, especially in businesses like law firms and small consulting firms, so value added per professional is a valuable measurement only if the profit figures can be purged of such items.

STABILITY

AVERAGE AGE

Older people are more stable employees than younger people because they tend not to leave a company. An organization with an older group of professionals is likely to be more stable than a younger organization in the same industry. Thus, average age is a good indicator of stability. And like turnover and seniority, it is also an indicator of dynamics: a high average age indicates a stable company with more wisdom than drive.

As described in Chapter 6, a company's average age has a habit of creeping upward unless management is alert. A steadily increasing average age over a long period of time is a warning sign. With the aid of a deliberate recruitment policy, it is possible to maintain a stable age structure, however.

Thanks to its growth and other active measures, *Affärsvärlden* managed to keep the age curve under control throughout the 1980s and until 1991, when editorial staff had to be cut. The average length of professional experience was also kept at a steady, fairly high level. Figure 24 illustrates this.

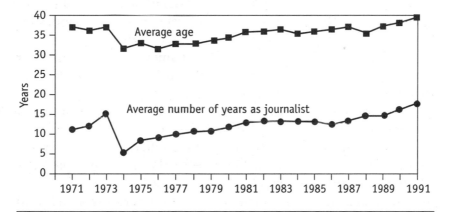

Figure 24. The "age" and "experience" curves are important in knowledge organizations and must be closely monitored. The average number of years is an indicator of professional competence.

Keeping the age and the experience of the professionals in balance is not easy. As Figure 24 shows, the curse of zero–growth–a rapidly aging staff–is never far off. During the years 1989 to 1991, when Sweden was hit by a severe recession, *Affärsvärlden* stopped growing and the average age immediately curved upward.

SENIORITY

Seniority is defined as the number of years employed in the same organization. The seniority of professionals is an indicator of stability of competence. The seniority of administrators can indicate the stability of the internal structure. (For more on this, see the "Rookie Ratio" section later in this chapter.)

RELATIVE PAY POSITION

Most industries and professional bodies keep good statistics on pay levels and the relative positions of individual companies. Relative pay position is usually expressed in index form, like 97 or 103; this has high information value because it measures relative cost levels compared with the competition. It can also be assumed to influence the attitudes of professionals on the payroll. Relative pay position is also of interest because it can indicate if employees are likely to look for work elsewhere.

PROFESSIONAL TURNOVER RATE

Staff turnover is generally regarded as an indicator of stability and is easy to calculate and compare with other companies. A very low turnover (below 5 percent) suggests a stable but static situation. A high turnover rate (above 20 percent) usually suggests that people are dissatisfied. The turnover rate should remain within a band; sudden change in the rate is usually an indication that something has changed internally in the company. Companies can use the turnover rate measure as a management tool to sustain a sufficient level of dynamics (see the WM–data case in Chapter 11).

The turnover rate is usually calculated as follows: the number of "leavers" during a year is divided by the number of people employed at the beginning of the year. The turnover rate can be more or less sophisticated; it can be divided into external turnover (people leaving the company) and internal turnover (job rotation) or, as suggested here, into the turnover rate for professionals and administrative staff.

ꞏꞌ Measuring the Internal Structure

The main activity of those employees who work in general management, administration, accounting, personnel, reception, clerical departments, and so on is to maintain the internal structure. These people make up the support staff. Those who carry out activities like routine maintenance of computer systems and databases should also be included among this group, unless their work refers to a specific customer or group of customers.

As when measuring competence, there are three measurement indicators for the internal structure: growth/renewal, efficiency, and stability.

GROWTH/RENEWAL

INVESTMENT IN THE INTERNAL STRUCTURE

Investments in new subsidiaries or new methods and systems are cash outlays that are often accounted for as costs. Such investments indicate a buildup of the internal structure and should be monitored and reviewed on a yearly basis. These investments can be represented as a proportion of sales or—better—a percentage of value added. (See Table 6 in Chapter 13.)

INVESTMENT IN INFORMATION PROCESSING SYSTEMS

Investment in information technology influences the internal structure. In many industries this investment is also regarded as a measure of progress toward accomplishing the corporate mission. An insurance company with more advanced IT systems can solve its customers' problems more efficiently. An airline with a sophisticated ticket booking system enjoys a competitive advantage over other airlines. Companies with systems for information retrieval and distribution have a powerful structure that supports the organization.

Thus, IT investments, expressed as percentages of sales (see the Celemi example, again, in Table 6) or in absolute figures, can provide valuable clues as to how the internal structure is developing. The number of computers or other IT packages per person can also be used as a control figure.

CUSTOMERS CONTRIBUTING TO INTERNAL STRUCTURE

The proportion of assignments devoted to customers that improve the internal structure of the company is an important variable because it adds to the growth of the asset. Examples include large projects where competence is passed on by tradition to several professionals at once. Innovative projects involving new materials, new methods of calculation, new software, and so on all fall under the heading of R&D and should be classed as such. However, customers too must be classified under this indicator. Two such classifications are illustrated in the cases of PLS–Consult and Celemi in Chapter 13.

EFFICIENCY

PROPORTION OF SUPPORT STAFF

The proportion of support staff to total number of employed is an indication of the efficiency of the internal structure. A change in the proportion indicates if the efficiency is improving.

SALES PER SUPPORT PERSON

Sales per support person can indicate how large a sales volume the organization's internal structure can handle. A change in the proportion indicates if efficiency is improving. (Table 6 in Chapter 13 illustrates this indicator.)

VALUES AND ATTITUDE MEASUREMENTS

Even though value judgments are usually a component of competence, one type of value judgment may be classified under the internal structure: the attitude of employees toward the workplace, customers, and superiors. This kind of attitude is often referred to as corporate culture or esprit de corps.

The employees' attitudes to their place of work can be measured just as the market's opinion of the company can be measured. If those attitudes are favorable, they contribute consciously or unconsciously to enhancing the company's image among its customers. If unfavorable, those attitudes will unconsciously influence customers and perhaps nullify the arguments of the most elaborate advertising campaign. How much of total marketing costs are nullified in this way by a company's own staff? Many companies, especially big ones, run regular polls to detect changes in employee attitudes. The results of such polls indicate how the internal structure is developing.

The results from attitude polls should be summarized in a few indices, which are then followed up yearly. It is imperative that the statistical methods used remain consistent from year to year because the change, rather than the absolute level, is of most interest.

STABILITY

AGE OF THE ORGANIZATION

An old organization is generally more stable than a young one. Retailers often post signs such as "Established 1887" to indicate to passersby that the shop is a trustworthy one. Corporate age is easy to compare with competitors.

SUPPORT STAFF TURNOVER

The support staff and the managers are the backbone of the internal structure. It is vital for the survival and efficiency that they function well, and a low turnover rate indicates this. The turnover rate for the staff should remain within a band, just like the rate for professionals. But because the objective of support staff is to maintain the internal structure, a lower turnover rate than for professionals is preferable; between 3 percent and 7 percent is probably best. (Again, Table 6 in Chapter 13 illustrates this indicator.)

THE ROOKIE RATIO

The "rookie ratio" is determined by the number of people with less than two years' employment. This group usually has a high personnel turnover. Its members are also less efficient than others because they have not yet been socialized into the tradition of the organization and do not know the most efficient way around. A high percentage of rookies is therefore a sign that the organization is less stable and less efficient.

The rookie ratio and seniority ratio complement each other. The two indicators can be used in tandem. (Table 6 in Chapter 13 illustrates this indicator.)

ᴵ Measuring the External Structure

The external structure includes brand names, image, and relationships with suppliers, but most importantly, it involves customer relationships. All the time that employees spend working for customers is potentially time for maintaining, building, and developing relations with customers. The professionals spend most of their time—maybe as much as 90 percent—on knowledge conversion, many of them in very intense cooperation with customers, others in backstage positions.

If all customers were profitable and also helped to develop competence, enhance image, and generate new assignments, a company would be very successful indeed. But of course they are not. Consequently, before measuring the growth/renewal, efficiency, and stability of the external structure, a company's customers must be categorized. Changes over time in the structure of this categorization can help companies assess their potential for development.

CATEGORIZING CUSTOMERS

To categorize customers, traditional financial statements can be supplemented with a statement showing customers grouped by categories. The Danish management consulting firm PLS–Consult maintains a knowledge–focused strategy and has begun to measure the competencies and development of its own staff as well as the ways in which its customers contribute invisible revenues. PLS thus presents a good illustration of how to categorize customers.

PLS divides its customers as follows:

- Those who contribute to image, references, and/or new assignments (rated on a scale as very much/average/not much). Such customers are either opinion leaders in their industry or so satisfied with PLS—or both—that they are willing to act as references.
- Those with challenging and widely educational projects that contribute to the firm's internal structure (very much/average/not much). The complex projects for these customers involve teams with many consultants who learn from one another. Some such projects are also staffed with consultants who are good at transferring skills to others. Customers that provide opportunities to develop new methods also belong in this category.
- Those who improve individual competence (very much/average/not much). Smaller customers with challenging assignments for only one consultant fall into this category.

The customers who belong to the "very much" class in all three categories total 15 percent of the firm's clients. These are the most valuable customers and the group that PLS wants to increase.

PLS also divides its consultants into three categories: those with less than three years' experience, between three and seven years' experience, and over seven years' experience. More than half its consultants have over seven years of experience. The basic qualification for employment is a bachelor's degree in engineering or business administration. PLS also seeks to classify its employees:

- Leaders competent at managing major projects
- Teachers competent at transferring skills to others working on a project (thus contributing to the internal structure)
- Generators competent at bringing in new customers

About half of PLS employees possess one or more of these abilities, which is a high proportion. Most of these findings are based on subjective assessments made by senior executives at PLS. Internal attitude surveys and customer satisfaction polls have also been carried out and will be repeated systematically in future.

These kinds of data enable PLS to keep its strategy under constant review. How much of its revenue, for example, comes from image? How much from educational customers? What proportion of its most valuable skills is being assigned to customers that can enhance the firm's image? How much of the revenue comes from very satisfied customers? Who are the most and the least satisfied customers? Which customers are most profitable in cash terms? How much revenue comes from the bread–and–butter customers that contribute financial profit but nothing else?

The management has identified the need for more teachers to enable PLS to grow faster. But how can actual and potential teachers be developed and recruited? And what kind of customer projects should such people be assigned to? By measuring the growth of volume in projects in which teachers are involved, the company can judge if it is on the right track. PLS would also like to win more image-enhancing customers. By measuring the volume of that segment, they can see the extent to which that goal is being achieved. Customer polls can thus be used for strategic purposes.

Satisfied customers are all–important, so the key to sustained profitability is establishing and maintaining stable customer relationships. Regular customer surveys offer moving pictures of customer satisfaction. A summary of responses to such a survey is shown in Figure 25.

The value of a customer base can also be assessed in terms of market development, because if customers are likely to generate a

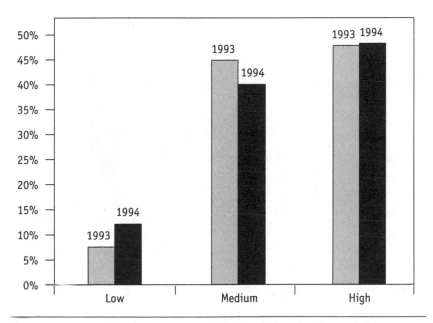

Figure 25. An issue of concern: The share of fees coming from highly satisfied customers is the same as last year, whereas the share of fees from the least satisfied customers has increased. A chart of this kind should raise some questions among the board.

flow of new projects rather than the occasional one–off, they are clearly more valuable. One of the most important means of competition is thus choosing the right customers. PLS distinguishes four categories of clients:

1. Customers who are profitable.
2. Customers who increase the competence of the engineers.
3. Customers who support the buildup of internal structure.
4. Customers who build up the image and provide contacts with other customers.

Of these categories, 2, 3, and 4 correspond to PLS's customer classification described earlier. Obviously some customers fall into more than one category, so the total adds to more than 100 percent. A key strategic aim is to attract customers whose projects will improve image, internal structure, or individual competence and will be high quality and profitable.

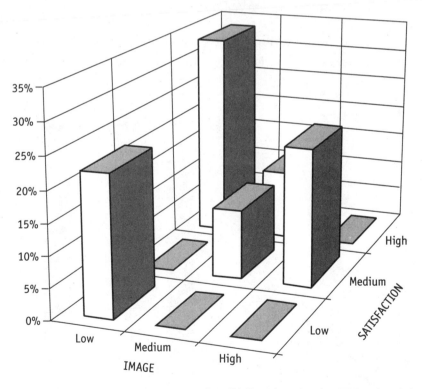

Note: This figure is not based on PLS-Consult statistics.

Figure 26. Strong efforts are put into low-image projects while the share of fees coming from high-quality projects, which give high image, is low.

Figure 26 shows that PLS is earning no revenue from satisfied high-image customers. If the firm is to gain image, something must be done about the situation. The goal is to achieve a distribution more like that shown in Figure 27.

High-image projects are both the best and the worst: they are the best if the customer is impressed by the high quality of the work and they are the worst if the customer is dissatisfied. If projects help develop new concepts and methods, or educate many employees, they are more valuable than other projects. Customers who provide opportunities for such projects help to reinforce the company's internal structure.

Once customers are categorized, indicators measuring growth/renewal, efficiency, and stability can once again be applied.

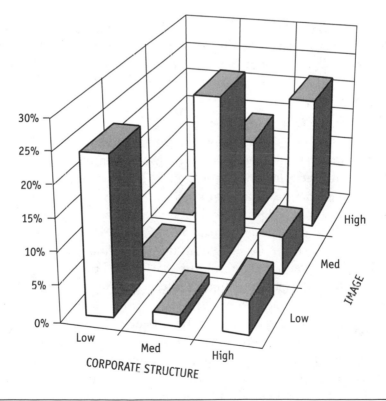

Figure 27. A good situation: almost 25% of revenues come from customers who also contribute significantly to both external image and corporate structure.

GROWTH/RENEWAL

PROFITABILITY PER CUSTOMER

When companies determine the profitability of their customer base, they often find to their dismay that up to 80 percent of their customer sales are not profitable. There is often surprisingly little information in companies on the profitability of customers because the costs are not accrued to customers but to products or functions. Customer profitability should be monitored routinely. To calculate the control figure—profitability per customer—costs and revenues must be categorized. This is a much more valuable criterion than profitability per product or market segment.

ORGANIC GROWTH

Organic growth, that is, an increase in billings with income from acquisitions deducted, is a measure of how well a business concept is received by the market. As discussed earlier in this book, purchased growth—growth from corporate acquisitions—is not necessarily a sign of success. It may be such a sign if the acquisition was a disguised mass recruitment of a group of professionals. But if a knowledge company grows by buying companies in other lines of business, it may actually be a sign that the original business concept is no longer generating enough growth.

EFFICIENCY

THE SATISFIED CUSTOMERS INDEX

The best early indication of whether results are about to improve or deteriorate is customer satisfaction. Many companies nowadays systematically acquire information about their customers' perceptions of quality and other attitudes about the company. The results of these polls are used primarily in marketing but rarely in financial forecasting. Yet it is perfectly feasible to append an index of customers' quality perceptions and attitudes to the financial statements.

There are several methods on the market for attempting to measure customer satisfaction. An index of this type need not be sophisticated to provide valuable information. Simple attitude polls can usually tell a lot. They need only be repeated at regular intervals, always with the same procedure and the same definitions, so that comparisons can be made and trends estimated. Results from these polls should be cross-analyzed with profitability data or efficiency indicators, as in the PLS–Consult example presented in the previous section.

WIN/LOSS INDEX

If a large portion of a company's business comes from bidding, it can calculate a simple index by comparing the number of successful bids with the number of unsuccessful ones. Compared over time this gives a good indication of how its customers regard it. The index can also be used for comparisons when trying out different pricing strategies.

SALES PER CUSTOMER

Because selling more to the same customer is usually easier and less costly than finding a new customer, this ratio measures the efficiency of a company's existing network of customers. An effort to expand the sales per customer should therefore be profitable. (An example is given in the Celemi case in Chapter 13.)

STABILITY

PROPORTION OF BIG CUSTOMERS

If a company's dependence on a few large customers is great, its position is weak and so is its structure. Two key indicators can measure this: percentage of billings attributable to the five biggest customers or number of customers accounting for 50 percent of billings. (Again, Table 6 in Chapter 13 provides an example.)

AGE STRUCTURE

Age structure—in this case, customer longevity—can also provide interesting information. The longer customers have been with a firm, the better its relations with them are likely to be and the easier it ought to be to retain them. The age structure usually changes only slowly.

DEVOTED CUSTOMERS RATIO

What proportion of sales comes from companies that have been customers for longer than five years? This measure indicates how devoted the customers are and therefore is a sign of stability. Naturally, a startup company will have a low ratio.

FREQUENCY OF REPEAT ORDERS

Another measure of customer satisfaction is the frequency of repeat orders. A high frequency indicates that customers are satisfied. And since old customers, as a rule, are more profitable than new ones, this key indicator also tells something about profitability potential.

The willingness of customers to place repeat orders is a further indication of customer-perceived quality and whether the company has found the right customer base. Stable, loyal customers are profitable customers in the long term. If customer utility is high, so are earnings.

The frequency of repeat orders can be measured as the proportion of total billings attributable to old customers. The meaning of *old* naturally varies according to the type of business, but normally a customer who has given at least one previous assignment can be regarded as an old customer. (An example is again in Table 6 in Chapter 13.)

Summary

- The first step in designing a measurement system for intangible assets is to understand the system's purpose and audience.
- The second step is to classify employee groups by type.
- The measurements for each of the three intangible assets can be grouped into those indicating growth and renewal, efficiency, or stability.
- Under the competence grouping, only professionals are measured. Their work should be measured according to the type of activity, degree of responsibility, or area.
- Under the internal structure grouping, only the support staff is measured. Under the external structure grouping, the time employees spend maintaining, building, and developing customer relations is measured.
- Customers should be classified, too, based on the intangible asset they provide—such as image, learning, and references—as well as on their profitability.

Implementing Systems for
Measuring Intangible Assets

The debate about how to account for intangible assets has been gathering momentum all over the world in recent years, centering on the question of how to create a written account of the goodwill resulting from corporate acquisitions. The debate was spurred by widely publicized purchases at the end of the 1980s of consumer-goods groups that were rich in brands and trademarks. In the 1990s the focus of the debate has shifted to the assets routinely referred to by company chairmen as "our greatest," that is, employees.

This chapter presents several case studies of companies that have implemented measuring systems for their intangible assets and reported the results publicly. It concludes with some general guidelines for creating a measurement system.

✒ Public Reporting in Sweden and Denmark

Sweden has taken the lead in publishing personnel statements. Annual reports nowadays, especially of public companies, usually contain a page or two of key figures and graphs on the subject, most of them based on the recommendations in *Den Osynliga Balansräkningen (The Invisible Balance Sheet*, Sveiby et al. 1989).

No such figures appear in the annual reports of companies in other countries. Even the world's largest knowledge companies, such as computer consultants EDS and Cap Gemini Sogeti, provide no more than a few hints that they employ human beings. One can only suspect that the woeful lack of relevant information—as in Microsoft's annual reports—represents a lack of understanding of the economics of knowledge and competence.

Two Swedish firms, WM–data and Skandia AFS, are international leaders in this field and have approached the subject in two different ways. WM–data has measured intangible assets for over a decade. It has included a comprehensive section on the subject in its annual reports ever since 1989 and, with six years of experience using these indicators, it is a pioneer in the field. The indicators have been used to follow WM–data's strategy (discussed in Chapter 11), but the company has maintained a low profile in its public reporting.

Skandia AFS (a subsidiary of the Skandia insurance group) has chosen to make the measurement of intangible assets a differentiation device. It appointed a "director of intellectual capital" in 1990, whose job it was to devise a way to depict intellectual capital. Skandia now has three years of experience. The company actively and publicly promotes its Business Navigator, which incorporates a large number of key indicators and is one of the driving forces in the intellectual capital movement.

WM-DATA'S 1995 ANNUAL REPORT

The section entitled "How Our Capital Is Managed" in WM–data's annual report occupies five pages with graphs and explanatory text.[1] These are shown in Exhibit 10.

WM–data follows my recommendations (which I first outlined in 1988), dividing its intangible assets into the three categories suggested in the present work.

1. WM–data's *internal structure* includes its esprit de corps, competence development, management operations, office furnishings, the special status conferred to consultants, and a feeling of security that comes from working for a stable company.

2. Its *external structure* is composed of employee ability to establish and maintain good relations with the outside world. Being a maker and upholder of contacts confers high status at WM–data.

3. *Competence*, or in WM–data's terms, individual capital, is cultivated by bringing family members into the corporate fellowship and through competence development. WM–data maintains that stability on the personnel side contributes to stability in customer relations.

SKANDIA'S PROCESS MEASUREMENTS

The report on its intangible assets issued by Skandia AFS has attracted international attention. It is the result of a program headed by the company's intellectual capital director, Leif Edvinsson. This program too is based on concepts presented in Sveiby et al. (1988,

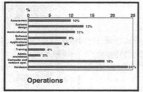

Operations

releases. The intention is to gradually add more operative information about customers, products, employees and services. In the future it will also be possible to make financial and capacity utilisation reports via the network. It is already clear that WM-data's Intranet will play a vital role as bearer of the corporate culture and

Industry

information channel in the Company's continued expansion.

Customers are the other cornerstone of the structural capital. WM-data's philosophy is not only to create good results for our customers, but also to develop relationships. WM-data has long relationships with a number of its customers, in certain cases, for example with Statoil,

Markets

lasting since the very start more than 25 years ago.

Public administrations, retail and distribution, and industry account for approximately one-third each of WM-data's revenue. Sweden accounted for 87 per cent of revenue in 1995. The increase of six percentage points compared with 1994 was mainly attributable to the acquisition of Owell.

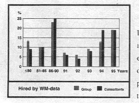

Hired by WM-data ■ Group ■ Consultants

Individual Capital

Individual capital is the knowledge and ability of each employee. In 1995, the number of

Social unity is highly important in a knowledge-based company. For several years, it has been a tradition for employees and customers to

employees rose from 2,080 to 3,040. Of these, Owell and other acquisitions accounted for 680. The remainder, approximately 500 employees, were recruited in 1995 and 220 employees left the Company during the year.

This dramatic increase was possible thanks to the fact that WM-data has no staff functions such as a personnel department. Instead, recruitment is the responsibility of the individual group and unit managers.

From the start, the Company has worked to keep administration to a minimum. The proportion of administrative personnel may not exceed ten per cent. This not only keeps costs

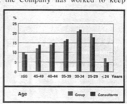

Age ■ Group ■ Consultants

Exhibit 10. From WM-data's 1995 annual report.

get together at Bern's in Stockholm on the last Wednesday of each month to socialise in an informal environment.

down, it also contributes to greater flexibility.

In a knowledge-based company, revenue and income are directly related to the number of revenue-earning employees. If demand and prices are constant, income can only be increased through the addition of more revenue-earning employees.

At year-end 1995, WM-data had 2,700 revenue-earning employees, compared with 1,900 the year before.

Loyal, skilled and motivated staff are the best guarantee for achieving good results. Stability among employees creates stability among customers. This is only possible through an over-all approach to the employees. Only employees who receive understanding at home for their professional efforts at WM-data have the potential to make a positive contribution both at work and at home. That is why family members are included in the WM-data community.

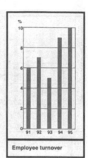

Employee turnover

However, all organisations benefit from a certain level of staff turnover, which has a revitalising effect on the organisation. WM-data aims for an annual staff turnover of ten per cent, which was the outcome in 1995. Today the Company is so large that there is also an internal labour market for those who wish to change working tasks or develop their expertise.

New recruitment has led to a younger workforce. The average age fell from 38 to 36 in 1995. A large portion of the new recruitment was drawn directly from universities and colleges, among other things in order to prevent the average age from creeping upwards. Nearly half of the employees are 34 or younger.

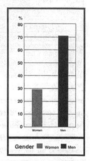

Gender ■ Women ■ Men

WM-data has thus created a better balance between highly experienced and relatively new employees. Sixty-six per cent of the employees have at least six years of professional experience. Many of the new recruits have also provided the Group with valuable skills in expansive areas, such the Internet and World Wide Web. This is of vital importance for the Company's continued development.

WM-data works determinedly to increase the proportion of women, and to interest more women in the consulting

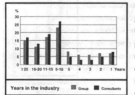

Years in the industry ■ Group ■ Consultants

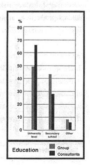

Education ■ Group ■ Consultants

Exhibit 10. (continued).

1989), but Skandia has taken them a step further by applying them to more areas than I suggested and incorporating ideas from *The Balanced Scorecard* (Kaplan and Norton 1996).

Skandia's Business Navigator incorporates a total of about thirty key indicators in various areas, which are monitored internally on a yearly basis. The areas are *financial focus, customer focus, process focus, human focus,* and *development/renewal focus,* as shown in Figure 28.

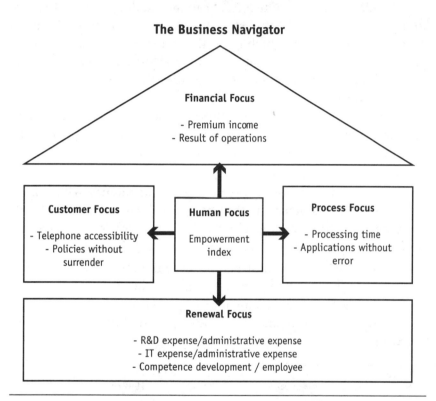

The Business Navigator

Financial Focus

- Premium income
- Result of operations

Customer Focus

- Telephone accessibility
- Policies without surrender

Human Focus

Empowerment index

Process Focus

- Processing time
- Applications without error

Renewal Focus

- R&D expense/administrative expense
- IT expense/administrative expense
- Competence development / employee

Figure 28. Some key indicators for Skandia AFS. Source: Company annual report, 1995, supplement on intellectual capital.

■ For Skandia, *customer focus* is the equivalent of the external structure category described in this book.

■ *Process focus* is the equivalent of the internal structure category.

■ *Human focus* is the equivalent of the competence category.

Each focus has its own key indicators:

■ Customer focus: number of accounts, number of brokers, number of lost customers

- Process focus: number of accounts per employee and administrative costs per employee
- Human focus: personnel turnover, proportion of managers, proportion of female managers, training/education costs per employee
- Development/renewal focus: satisfied employee index, marketing expense per customer, share of training hours

Skandia's report on intellectual capital is a document of twenty-four pages, which is distributed as a supplement to the 1995 annual report.[2] The document highlights the company's value—creating processes. Skandia does not measure performance of intangible assets as such, but many of the ratios are similar to the ones suggested in this book.

The program is probably the most ambitious in the world today. The implementation process has now reached the stage where the key indicators are to be used in day–to–day operations.

PLS-CONSULT'S VALUE ADDED

PLS–Consult is a Danish management consultancy with a large proportion of customers in the service industries. In its 1993–94 annual report the company delineated its intangible assets.[3] They are divided into three classes, as recommended in this book:

- *Customer capital* (external structure), described by turnover per category of client and importance of major clients
- *Intellectual knowledge* (competence), presented through the key indicators of academic qualifications and seniority among its consultants

PLS-Consult *(Amounts in thousands of Danish kronor)*	1991/92	1992/93	1993/94
Net sales	27,144	28,936	39,850
Extraordinary expenditure	6,486	6,415	10,640
Other external expenditure	3,514	3,667	4,691
Depreciation and write-offs	798	747	704
Total expenditure	10,798	10,829	16,035
Value added	16,346	18,107	23,815
Average number of full-time employees	42	51	62
Value added per employee	389	355	384

Table 5. Value added statement from PLS-Consult's annual report.

■ *Organizational knowledge* (internal structure), presented as a verbal description of the organization and its philosophy

The company's method of reporting value added is shown in Table 5.

▪ A Knowledge Audit of Celemi

In its 1995 annual report, Celemi, a Swedish company that develops and sells training tools, used a "knowledge audit" to present its intangible assets, the first time that a company ever did so. In an audit, the company opens its books for an outside expert who makes an assessment of the performance of the intangible assets based on the data that the company provides. The following text is extracted from the annual report. It should be noted that I was the author of this part of the annual report.

CELEMI'S INTANGIBLE ASSETS

Celemi's "invisible" balance sheet contains intangible assets that can be classified under three main headings:

Our Customers are an external structure of relationships with customers and suppliers as well as our brand names, trademarks, contracts, and reputation or image. This structure is constantly being created by Celemi's employees. The value of customer relations is primarily influenced by how well Celemi solves customer problems. Some of these structures are Celemi's legal property but their future value depends on customer confidence.

Our Organization is an internal corporate structure consisting of patents, concepts, vendor contracts, models, and computer and support systems, including for general management purposes. This structure is also a creation of Celemi's employees and its components are generally owned by Celemi. Decisions to develop or invest in the organization can be made with some degree of confidence because the work is done in-house or bought outside.

Our People represent the combined competence of Celemi's employees, including their ability to act in a wide variety of situations. The value of people is that they are the only true agents in business; all assets and structures, whether visible or invisible, are the result of human action and depend on competence and energy for their continued existence. People are, however, not a corporate asset like the two structures above because people cannot be owned.

The total commercial value of Celemi's intangible assets on December 31, 1995 can be estimated only with a great degree of uncertainty and it is pointless to do it here. It is clear however that Celemi's invisible balance sheet is much larger than our visible one. What is of great interest for Celemi's stakeholders is whether the intangible assets are increasing in value and whether they are utilized efficiently. This can be established with some certainty, and it is the aim of Celemi's Intangible Assets Monitor.

INVISIBLE REVENUES

Just as visible revenues improve the tangible equity, invisible revenues improve the efficiency and the value of Celemi's intangible assets. By canvassing customers who provide invisible revenues, rather than those that merely contribute money, Celemi is able to improve actively its intangible assets. One way to capture the impact is to calculate the proportion of revenues that comes from three categories of customers:

Image-enhancing customers, who improve Celemi's potential to find new customers or reduce the marketing costs involved. Such customers are well-regarded in their industries. References or testimonials from them are very valuable. Thus, they improve Celemi's external structure.

Organization-enhancing customers, who demand state-of-the art solutions that are new to Celemi and thus contribute to Celemi's R&D, or who have very large projects that involve many professionals and thus enable transfer of tacit competence. Such customers improve Celemi's internal structure.

Competence-enhancing customers, who bring projects challenging the competence of Celemi's employees. These customers are valuable because Celemi's employees learn from them.

OUR CUSTOMERS (EXTERNAL STRUCTURE)

Image-enhancing customers contributed 40 percent of Celemi's revenues in 1995, which is a very high proportion. These customers are large, well-known multinational corporations, with a high potential for further growth.

Our customers are loyal. One indicator of this is the level of repeat orders. No less than 66 percent of our customers in

1995 were with Celemi in 1994. Considering the rapid growth in revenues, this is a very high proportion indeed. A high level of repeat orders also indicates that canvassing costs can be kept low.

The most cost–efficient way to grow is to improve the sales per customer. In 1995 this measure grew by only 4 percent, which is too low.

The five largest customers account for 41 percent of our revenues, which is a large proportion. Celemi does not want to become too dependent on a few key customers, so the indicator should not be allowed to go much higher.

In sum, Celemi's external structure is probably the most valuable part of its intangible assets. It seems stable and with a large potential to generate invisible revenues in the future.

OUR ORGANIZATION (INTERNAL STRUCTURE)

Celemi is evolving from a small firm that is dependent on a few highly skilled and efficient senior individuals to a large corporation with an internal structure that can support a larger number of professionals and take on large projects on a global basis. This is an ambitious goal, and 1995 was the first year of transition for Celemi. To achieve this goal Celemi invested no less than 33 percent of value added in new products, IT, and new subsidiaries in 1995.

Customers contributed to this transition by entrusting Celemi with some very large projects and support for new products. Management estimates that some 44 percent of revenues in 1995 came from customers who enhance the structure of the organization, which is a very high proportion.

One effect of rapid growth is the low rate of seniority among the support staff, at present only three years. Another is the "rookie ratio"—the proportion of all people employed less than two years—which is a very high 64 percent. Both numbers indicate instability and high costs for recruiting and developing people in 1995. However, if these new people stay with the company, the numbers will improve in the coming years and reflect better stability.

Celemi's support staff handles fairly large volumes–in 1995, 7.6 MSEK per person. However, this was a decrease of 20 percent over 1994. The proportion of sales to support staff increased by only 4 percent. Both numbers reflect investment in new staff and indicate that Celemi now has support capacity for future growth.

In sum, Celemi's new organization does not yet seem stable and is not yet up to full efficiency. However, it has a high potential for volume growth and efficiency improvement in the coming years.

OUR PEOPLE (COMPETENCE)

These indicators in the Intangible Balance Sheet also show 1995 as a year of transition. Celemi had fifty employees on December 31, 1995—a full 92 percent more than in 1994. The total competence of all the experts—measured as years of professional experience—increased by 43 percent, which is significant.[4]

Celemi has been recruiting younger people primarily. The median age is now a healthy thirty-four years, down from thirty-nine in 1994. The average professional experience of the experts therefore declined by 25 percent, which normally would indicate problems in serving the customers. However, the average professional experience is still a high 7.8 years. Celemi has retained all the senior experts and the turnover among experts was a healthy 10 percent, indicating that Celemi's competence is still in good order despite the changes.

Celemi's people are well-educated. Two-thirds of our experts have a university degree. The average for all employees is between secondary (2) and tertiary (3) levels, with an average of 2.3, unchanged compared with last year. This is too low in light of management's goal to improve the educational level through recruiting.

The output of Celemi's people is quite high. The value added per expert was TSEK 867 in 1995, which is high in this particular industry, but it slipped by 13 percent over 1994; the value added per employee likewise declined by 13 percent. Again, this is a reflection of the organizational changes and the efficiency should improve in 1996.

Some 43 percent of total revenues in 1995 came from competence-enhancing customers, which is very important, particularly for the many new recruits.

Intangible Assets Monitor
1994–1995

Our Customers (External Structure)		**Our Organization** (Internal Structure)		**Our People** (Competence)	
Growth/Renewal		**Growth/Renewal**		**Growth/Renewal**	
Revenue growth	44%	IT investment percent value added[15]	11%	Avg. professional experience,[7] years	7.8 -25%
Image-enhancing customers[2]	40%	Organization-enhancing customers[2]	44%	Competence-enhancing customers[2]	43%
		Product R&D percent value added	18%	Total competence, experts,[4,7] years	298 43%
		Total investment in org. percent value added	33%	Average education level[3]	2.3 0%
Efficiency		**Efficiency**		**Efficiency**	
Change in sales per customer[12]	4%	Change proportion of admin. staff[1,8]	4%	Value added per expert,[4,15] TSEK	867 -13%
		Sales per admin. staff growth[6,11]	-20%	Value added per employee,[6,15] TSEK	665 -13%
Stability		**Stability**		**Stability**	
Repeat orders[9]	66%	Admin. staff turnover[1,14]	0%	Expert turnover[4,14]	10%
Five largest customers percent[5]	41%	Admin. staff seniority, years[1,13]	3	Expert seniority,[4,13] years	2.3 79%
		Rookie ratio[10]	64%	Median age all employees, years	34.0 -12%

Notes:
1. Administrative staff: All employees other than experts.
2. Customers: Categorized under three headings. The indicator is percent share of revenues.
3. Education level: Employees at year-end with primary education ("Grundskola," calculated as =1), secondary ("Gymnasium" =2), and Tertiary ("Universitet" =3).
4. Experts: Employees working directly with customers in projects. Top management are regarded as experts because they work actively with customers.
5. Five largest customers: Share of revenues from five largest customers.
6. Number of staff: Two definitions are used—average number employed during year for efficiency indicators; year-end numbers for growth/renewal and stability indicators.
7. Professional competence: Number of years in current profession.
8. Proportion of administrative staff: Number of administrative staff divided by number of total staff at year-end.
9. Repeat orders: Customers also existing in 1994 (those corresponding to two-thirds of revenues).
10. Rookie ratio: Number of employees with less than two years' seniority.
11. Sales per administrative staff: Total revenues divided by average number of administrative staff.
12. Sales per customer: Total revenues divided by average number of customers.
13. Seniority: Number of years as Celemi employees.
14. Staff turnover: Number of leavers divided by number of staff at beginning of year.
15. Value added: The value produced by Celemi's employees after payment to all outside vendors.

Table 6. The Intangible Assets Monitor, Celemi, Sweden. Source: Company annual report, 1995.

In sum, Celemi's rapid growth in people compared with previous years is a management accomplishment that will profoundly change and revitalize the company. The newcomers are well educated and on a steep learning curve.

◗ Why Isn't Intangibles Reporting More Widespread?

Alternative key indicators provide interesting new angles and are of great value to both investors and managers. Since the 1950s and earlier, companies have calculated some nonmonetary indicators to corroborate efficiency studies, but they never publish them in their annual reports.

There are several reasons for their coyness and for the lack of development in the measurement of intangible assets. One is that many managers regard such reporting as pointless. The only response they get to their annual reports comes from financial analysts, who usually leaf quickly past this kind of information because they do not know how to interpret the figures and have no time to learn how. Nor are managers aware of the internal uses. There are few corporate managements that—like those of WM–data, Skandia AFS, or PLS–Consult—understand how such calculations can be used to monitor operations.

Yet, the second reason is the antithesis of the first: the fear that such indicators might give too much away. Few companies dare publish information about who their customers are and what they think about the company, who their competitors are, or what their internal or external image is like. They may publish some figures if they look good, but the interesting figures, those that can be freely interpreted by independent commentators or might reveal some competitive advantage, are not willingly disclosed.

A third reason was already mentioned earlier in this book: there is no rigorous theoretical model for this type of report. Accounting systems are not designed for the purpose, which makes the key indicators difficult and expensive to develop and impossible to compare.

Thus, it is hard to mobilize the pressure from the authorities and the investors that is needed to make managers publish figures that show them at a disadvantage. Legal rules and public opinion are very important when it comes to reporting. The requirements annual reports must now meet are the result of past action by various pressure groups. But the response to Skandia's intellectual capital report suggests that the time is ripe for change.

▪ Creating and Monitoring a Knowledge-Focused Strategy

Exhibit 11 summarizes the action steps to take and the tools to measure a knowledge-focused strategy.

▪ The Intangible Assets Monitor

The Intangible Assets Monitor is a presentation format that displays a number of relevant indicators in a simple fashion. An example of the monitor is shown in Exhibit 12.

The choice of indicators depends on the company's strategy. As the cases of PLS–Consult, WM–data, and Celemi show, the indicators can and should be used to follow up a more knowledge-focused strategy.

The Intangible Assets Monitor can be integrated into the management information system. It should not exceed one page in length but should be accompanied by a number of comments. The purpose of a measuring system is to cover all intangible assets, so an individual company should select only a few of the suggested measurement indicators for each intangible asset. The most important areas to cover are growth and renewal, efficiency, and stability.

▪ Moving Toward a Knowledge-Focused Strategy

My goal in this book has been to help my readers understand and make the best of what I believe are among the most important of the profound and confusing changes taking place in the modern business environment.

My method has been to urge all to look consciously at these changes and their own organizations from what I call the knowledge perspective. It is my belief that only those who understand the subtle differences between knowledge and information and have a feel for the strange markets they are encountering will be equipped to exploit the opportunities and circumvent the dangers that lie ahead.

Why is it necessary to look *consciously*? Because so much of what we do, day to day, is governed by attitudes and unconscious rules that obscure our vision. Why a *knowledge perspective*? Because knowledge is the ultimate wellspring of unlimited resources and it is crucial for us to understand what knowledge is and what it is not. The common, unconscious assumption that knowledge is simply another word for information is false and dangerous. A far more accurate and helpful assumption for businesspeople is that information is useless. Information-based strategies are relatively unsophisticated and thus

Action to Take	Relation to Intangible Asset	Way to Monitor
MANAGE COMPETENCE	BENEFIT	INDICATOR TO USE
Carefully recruit bright young people who are easy to indoctrinate.	Provides inflow of new fresh competence and energy; strengthens culture	Rookie ratio, divided into university-educated rookies and other rookies
Improve the education level among all employees.	Increases flexibility and learning rate	Education levels
Offer careers that are up-or-out; no plateaus allowed.	Individuals encouraged to maintain steep learning curve or leave; creates turnover	Individual grading; average marks
Make competence maps.	Identifies competencies	Number of people in each category, of years in profession
Use juniors as assistants.	Enables tradition of tacit knowledge; reduces administration	Proportion of junior time spent for competence-enhancing customers
Keep people from leaving by creating loyalty.	Competence is not lost to competition	Attitude surveys; staff turnover
Build close personal relations with a few selected clients.	Creates inflow of knowledge	Proportion of competence-enhancing customers
Let young learn from old in master/apprentice relationships.	Enables tradition of tacit knowledge	Attitude surveys
MANAGE THE INTERNAL STRUCTURE	BENEFIT	INDICATOR TO USE
Go for large assignments that allow teams.	Teams allow tradition of tacit knowledge among members	Proportion of organization-improving customers
Develop own concepts and methods.	Creates of new knowledge, R&D	Time devoted to R&D
Publicize the concepts in books and seminars.	Influences the mindsets of potential customers; creates standards	Time devoted to such activities

Exhibit 11. An action plan for implementing and measuring a knowledge-focused strategy.

Create information-sharing system.	Supports knowledge combination	Investment level in IT
Charge for teams, not for individuals.	Conceals the elevated fees of the seniors; reduces internal competition; improves tradition	Proportion of team billing
Proactively manage age structure	Reduces risk for plateaus, keeps balance between dynamic and static forces	Median age; staff turnover
Build close personal relations with customers that provide R&D projects or large projects.	Improves internal structure and enables learning	Proportion of organization-improving customers
Encourage piggybacking in all departments.	Enables tradition of tacit knowledge	Proportion of junior time spent for competence-enhancing customers
Organize departments as open-space offices.	Enables tradition of tacit knowledge	Attitude surveys; proportion of open-space offices
Communicate mission for business.	Gives focus and purpose of knowledge creation	Attitude surveys
MANAGE THE EXTERNAL STRUCTURE	**BENEFIT**	**INDICATOR TO USE**
Focus management information on customers rather than markets or products.	Knowledge flows through relations, not through markets	Proportion of image-enhancing customers
Build image as "USA's most competent in your industry segment" by giving seminars, etc.	Reduces marketing costs	Number of seminars held; customer surveys
Select customers that contribute to intangible assets or profit; cut out the rest.	Concentrates efforts to most valuable customers; improves inflow of knowledge	Categorize customers, compute profitability, sales per customer
Build teams with customer chemistry in mind.	Improves success rate and inflow of knowledge	Win/loss index; satisfied customers index
Nurture image as an important asset.	Reduces marketing costs	Money spent, time used; satisfied customers index
Treat former employees as honored alumni.	Retains relationships that enhance instead of damage image; can also lead to new customer relationships	Alumni surveys

Intangible Assets

External Structure	Internal Structure	Competence of People
Growth/Renewal	**Growth/Renewal**	**Growth/Renewal**
Organic volume growth. Growth in market share. Satisfied customer index or quality index.	Investments in IT. Share of time devoted to internal R&D activities. Attitude index of personnel toward managers, culture, customers.	Share of sales from competence-enhancing customers. Growth in average professional experience (number of years). Competence turnover.
Efficiency	**Efficiency**	**Efficiency**
Profit per customer. Sales per professional.	Proportion of support staff. Sales per support staff.	Change in added value per professional. Change in proportion of professionals.
Stability	**Stability**	**Stability**
Frequency of repeat orders. Age structure.	Age of the organization. Rookie ratio.	Turnover rate of professionals.

Exhibit 12. An example of an Intangible Assets Monitor.

easy to copy. There is really only one way to win in what I term the *informatized* markets: to be first and to run faster than everybody else.

But a number of intuitive managers have already discovered another track and are adopting knowledge-focused strategies. They have seen beyond the traditional commonsense criteria of organizational health and performance and dared to put their faith in nonmonetary indicators. A few such people were discussed in this book.

Although I have argued against the widespread notion that information is valuable, I am not saying information technology should be dispensed with. I am saying that it is dangerous to assume that the informatization of a business will give competitive advantage and lead to increasing returns. The decision to invest in IT is straightforward, so it is very likely that competitors will do the same. In contrast, the design of organizational spaces conducive to knowledge creation, for example, is much more difficult to accomplish and virtually impossible to copy because it exploits the value of the tacit, which is greater than the value of the explicit.

Knowledge-focused strategies are relatively intricate in that they are multifaceted and require both an intimate knowledge of and a willingness to empower people. Those who focus their attention on releasing the infinite capacity of humans to create knowledge have found many ways to exploit knowledge. But their approaches have been largely intuitive and relied on imagination and experiment.

The virtues of a knowledge focus are not limited to the business world, of course; they are an issue for society as a whole. Imagine what a more knowledge–focused approach would do to reduce costs in the public sector! Take health care, for example. The costs of medical care are rising rapidly and we are running out of ideas to make the system more efficient. Too many hospitals are still managed according to Taylor's scientific management principles like factories, with doctors acting as omnipotent experts, nurses as powerless workers, and patients as unintelligible raw material. Health care is inefficient and ineffective because the sector is not designed to take the intangible revenues into account. The focus is on tangible cost control, not on intangible revenue generation. People today are better educated than they were when the industrial age model was developed. A way to slow down the rise in medical costs, therefore, is to exploit this investment by delegating some responsibility for patient care to the patients themselves. From a societal point of view it makes little sense to invest heavily in human knowledge and then not allow people to use it.

Acceptance of a self–care or patient–empowerment principle would increase the options open to physicians and hospitals. They could sell their diagnostic skills as knowledge services in the traditional way—as knowledge products in the form of packaged pregnancy test kits, for example—or as a knowledge process, by teaching patients how to diagnose and treat themselves.

I hope all managers will look closely at the organizations I call knowledge organizations, not because they are the best (far from it) but because they probably represent the future of all organizations. A word of warning though. One cannot try to create a knowledge organization—or any other kind of organization for that matter—based on models because models are always unrealistic. They are, at best, approximate representations of their designers' tacit knowledge. I hope instead that my readers will try to "see," as I suggested earlier in the book, by using the concepts I presented as a language for dialogue and to treat the suggested indicators as vision–enhancing devices.

It is also important that people do not despair if at first they can make no sense of the indicators and are unable to assess the significance of changes in competence turnover, staff stability, customer profitability, and so on. There will soon come a time when most people will be hungry for the kind of data I propose and when such data will appear as a matter of routine in management accounts and annual reports. But this process is still in its early stages. It takes at least two years of experimenting before one begins to get a feel for it. As long as we are not tempted to believe we are measuring some kind of objective truth, we will be okay.

As I have already said, I do not believe the information contained in a book such as this can really change anything. The only valuable knowledge is that which equips us for action and that kind of knowledge is learned the hard way—by doing. This is why I much prefer simulations to books when transferring management knowledge. It is up to you, my readers, to interpret, apply, and test my ideas by acting on them and reflecting on the results. Only then will my information become knowledge.

Notes

CHAPTER 1

1. The terms *structural capital* and *individual capital* were coined in Sveiby et al. (1988).

2. I first used this family of three in *Den Nya Arsredovisningen* (*The New Annual Report* 1988). Adaptations of the three families have since become widely used in Scandinavia, and I have seen them used since 1993 in the United States and Canada without reference to a source.

3. A label, definition, or category understood as a "family" is applied on the basis of overlapping similarities, not on common properties (Wittgenstein 1995, 67). Organizations that fall within the knowledge organization category resemble each other but are also different. For instance, software firms, architectural firms, and management consulting firms share some similarities with each other, with software developers, and with R&D departments of larger firms.

CHAPTER 2

1. I use both the terms *knowledge organization* and *knowledge company* because many such organizations do not sell to the market but derive their revenues from budgets or taxes. Examples include human resource departments, R&D departments, government ministries, and agencies.

2. According to the European Observatory for SMEs, in OECD countries 90 percent of all those employed in the business and professional services sector work in offices with one hundred or fewer people. Few were founded before the 1970s.

3. Wittgenstein's "aspect-seeing" or "seeing as" is a powerful notion for understanding how concepts rule the way we understand the world. It is one of the most used but least understood notions. The social sciences would hardly exist were it not for aspect-seeing, since their primary goal is to let us see humans and human behavior from different aspects. Thomas Kuhn's paradigm concept builds on Wittgenstein's aspect-seeing.

CHAPTER 3

1. The language cannot be described without mentioning the use to which it is put. Concepts are so fluid that it is not possible to define them strictly. The only way to see that a concept is understood is by how it is used. This notion has vast implications for managers trying to capture the tacit knowledge of people into explicit terminology. We can only hope to capture a very small proportion (Wittgenstein 1995, 69–77).

2. Main contributors to my understanding of Polanyi's concept of knowledge were Rolf (1991) and Sanders (1988).

3. Polanyi is here inspired by Piaget, who describes knowledge formation in terms of assimilation and adaptation.

4. In comparison, Von Glasersfelt (1988, 234) summarizes the construc-
   tivist view: "All knowledge is tied to action and knowing an object
   or an event is to use it by assimilating it to an action scheme."

5. "An articulate assertion is composed of two parts: a sentence con-
   veying the content of what is asserted and a tacit act by which this
   sentence is asserted. The act of assertion is an act of tacit compre-
   hension, which relies altogether on the self-satisfaction of the person who performs it. Unless an assertion of fact is accompanied by
   some heuristic or persuasive feeling it is a mere form of words saying nothing" (Polanyi 1958, 254).

CHAPTER 7

1. See Chapter 3 in *The Knowledge-Creating Company* (Nonaka and Takeuchi
   1995) for more details.

2. *Harvard Business Review,* May–June 1996, p. 33.

3. From the Latin for "I touch." It is the root of words like "tangible,"
   "intangible," and "tangent."

CHAPTER 8

1. Third annual report, 1995, European Observatory for SMEs.

2. *Manager,* April 1995.

3. The term *pro-team* was coined by Tom Lloyd (1987).

CHAPTER 9

1. According to Kim Ferrier Wilson htm Ltd, stockbrokers, two-year
   beta values for software companies on the Sydney stock exchange in
   August 1996 were 1.2 on average, that is, they fluctuated 20 percent
   more than those on the Sydney stock exchange's All Ordinaries
   Index.

2. For a practical description of how knowledge organizations can
   attract customers, see Nicou, Ribbing, and Ading (1994).

CHAPTER 10

1. As mentioned in the preface, I joined *Affärsvärlden* as a partner and
   manager in 1979 and held both editorial and managerial positions
   until we sold the company in 1994.

2. Two-year beta values were calculated on August 2, 1996, for a sam-
   ple of ten software and business service companies listed on the Sydney stock exchange.

CHAPTER 11

1. Competence is "owned" by the individual because no one can own
   a person. The issue of how to convert individual ownership into corporate intellectual property is not covered in this book.

2. "Momentum of Knowledge Management," Rogers 1996.
3. This interview appeared in *Business Review Weekly,* June 3, 1996.

CHAPTER 13

1. WM–data's annual report can be accessed via
   http://www.wmdata.com.
2. Skandia's annual report supplement can be accessed via
   http://www.skandia.se.
3. PLS–Consult's annual report can be accessed via http://www.pls.dk.
4. Celemi uses the term "expert" in the sense that I use "professional"
   in this book.

References

Arthur, W. Brian. 1996. "Increasing Returns and the New World of Business." *Harvard Business Review* 74 (July–Aug):100–109.

Argyris, Chris, and Donald Schön. 1978. *Organizational Learning*. Reading, Mass.: Addison–Wesley.

Brunsson, Nils. 1985. *The Irrational Organization: Irrationality as a Basis for Organizational Action and Change*. New York: Wiley.

"Cognitive Maps" (special issue) 1992. *Journal of Management Studies* 29 (May):261–389.

Coupland, Douglas. 1991. *Generation X: Tales for an Accelerated Culture*. New York: St. Martin's Press.

Cullen, Joe, and Jack Hollingum. 1987. *Implementing Total Quality*. Bedford, England: IFS Publications.

Czarniawska–Joerges, Barbara. 1993. *The Three-Dimensional Organization: A Constructionist View*. Lund: Studentlitteratur.

Davidow, William H., and Michael S. Malone. 1992. *The Virtual Corporation: Structuring and Revitalizing the Corporation for the 21st Century*. San Francisco: HarperCollins.

Drucker, Peter. 1993. *Post-Capitalist Society*. Oxford, England: Butterworth Heinemann.

Enstam, Nils, Ulf Johansson, and Marianne Nilson. 1995. *Sätt pris på förändringen*. Stockholm: Sveriges Verkstadsindustrier.

Glasersfeld, Ernst von. 1988. *The Construction of Knowledge: Contributions to Conceptual Semantics*. Salinas, Calif.: Intersystems Publications.

Grenier, Ray, and George Metes. 1992. *Enterprise Networking: Working Together Apart*. Bedford, Mass.: Digital Press.

Gröjer, Jane E., and Ulf Johanson. 1991. *Personalekonomisk redovisning och kalkylering*. Stockholm: Arbetarskyddsnvämnden (University of Stockholm).

Gummesson, Evert. 1996. "Relationship Marketing and Imaginary Organizations: A Synthesis." *European Journal of Marketing* 30, no. 2 (February):31–44.

Gustavsson, Bengt. 1992. *The Transcendent Organization: A Treatise on Consciousness in Organizations, Theoretical Discussion, Conceptual Development, and Empirical Studies*. Ph.D. diss., University of Stockholm.

Hall, Edward Twitchell. 1959. *The Silent Language*. Garden City, N.Y.: Doubleday.

Hamel, G., and C. K. Prahalad. 1990. "The Core Competence of the Corporation." *Harvard Business Review* 68 (May–June):79–91.

Hammer, Michael, and James Champy. 1993. *Reengineering the Corporation: A Manifesto for Business Revolution*. New York: HarperBusiness.

Handy, Charles B. 1989. *The Age of Unreason.* Boston: Harvard Business School Press.

Hedberg, Bo, G. Dahlgren, J. Jansson, and N-G. Olve. 1994. *Imaginary Organizations.* Malmö: Liber Hermod.

Jantsch, Erich. 1980. *Self-Organizing Universe: Scientific and Human Implications of the Emerging Paradigm.* New York: Pergamon Press.

Johansen, Robert, and Rob Swigart. 1994. *Upsizing the Individual in the Downsized Organization: Managing in the Wake of Reengineering, Globalization, and Overwhelming Technological Change.* Reading, Mass.: Addison-Wesley.

Johansen, Robert et al. 1991. *Leading Business Teams: How Teams Can Use Technology and Group Process Tools to Enhance Performance.* Reading, Mass.: Addison-Wesley.

Johanson, Ulf, and Marianne Nilson. 1990a. *Personalekonomiska beräkningar.* Ph.D. diss., University of Stockholm.

Johanson, Ulf, and Marianne Nilson. 1990b. *Personalekonomi en litteraturstudie.* Ph.D. diss., University of Stockholm.

Johanson, Ulf, and Marianne Nilson. 1996. "The Usefulness of Human Resource Costing and Accounting." *Journal of Human Resource Costing and Accounting* 1, no. 1:117–138.

Kanter, Rosabeth Moss. 1983. *The Change Masters: Innovation and Entrepreneurship in the American Corporation.* New York: Simon & Schuster.

Kanter, Rosabeth Moss. 1989. *When Giants Learn to Dance: Mastering the Challenge of Strategy, Management, and Careers in the 1990's.* New York: Simon & Schuster.

Kaplan, Robert, and David Norton. 1996. *The Balanced Scorecard: Translating Strategy into Action.* Boston: Harvard Business School Press.

Kuhn, Thomas. [1962] 1986. *The Structure of Scientific Revolutions.* Reprint. New York: New American Library.

Leinberger, Paul, and Bruce Tucker. 1991. *The New Individualists: The Generation After the Organization Man.* New York: HarperCollins.

Lloyd, Tom. 1990. *The 'Nice' Company.* London: Bloomsbury.

Masuda, Yoneji. 1980. *The Information Society as Post-Industrial Society.* Tokyo: Institute for the Information Society and Sweden: Informationssamhället, Liber.

McLuhan, Marshall. 1967. *Understanding Media: The Extensions of Man.* London: Routledge & Kegan Paul.

Mintzberg, Henry. 1983. *Structures in Fives: Designing Effective Organizations.* Englewood Cliffs, N.J.: Prentice-Hall.

Mintzberg, Henry. 1978. "Patterns in Strategy Formation," *Management Science* 24 (May):934–948.

Naisbitt, John. 1982. *Megatrends: Ten New Directions Transforming Our Lives.* New York: Warner Books.

Nicou, Monica, Christine Ribbing, and Eva Ading. 1994. *Sell Your Knowledge: The Professional's Guide to Winning More Business.* London: Kogan Page.

Nonaka, Ikujiro, and Hirotaka Takeuchi. 1995. *The Knowledge-Creating Company*. Oxford: Oxford University Press.

Nørretranders, Tor. 1993. *Märk Världen*. Stockholm: Bonnier.

Pascale, Richard. 1990. *Managing on the Edge: How the Smartest Companies Use Conflict to Stay Ahead*. New York: Simon & Schuster.

Peters, Thomas. 1992. *Thriving on Chaos: Handbook for a Management Revolution*. New York: Knopf.

Pinchot, Gifford, and Elizabeth Pinchot. 1995. *The End of Bureaucracy and the Rise of the Intelligent Organization*. San Francisco: Berrett–Koehler.

Polanyi, Michael. 1958. *Personal Knowledge: Towards a Post-Critical Philosophy*. London: Routledge & Kegan Paul.

Polanyi, Michael. 1967. *The Tacit Dimension*. London: Routledge & Kegan Paul.

Porter, Michael E. 1980. *Competitive Strategy: Techniques for Analyzing Industries and Competitors*. New York: Free Press.

Quinn, James Brian. 1992. *Intelligent Enterprise: A Knowledge and Service Based Paradigm for Industry*. New York: Free Press.

Rheingold, Howard. 1993. *The Virtual Community: Homesteading on the Electronic Frontier*. Reading, Mass.: Addison–Wesley.

Ritzer, George. 1993. *The McDonaldization of Society: An Investigation into the Changing Character of Contemporary Social Life*. Newbury Park, Calif.: Pine Forge Press.

Rogers, Debra M. Amidon. 1996. "Knowledge Management Gains Momentum in Industry." *Research-Technology Management* 39 (May/June):5–7.

Rolf, Bertil. 1991. *Profession Tradition Och Tyst Kunskap*. Sweden: Doxa.

Sanders, Andy F. 1988. *Michael Polanyi's Post-Critical Epistemology: A Reconstruction of Some Aspects of "Tacit Knowing."* Amsterdam: Rodopi.

Savage, Charles. 1996. *Fifth Generation Management: Co-creating through Virtual Enterprising, Dynamic Teaming, and Knowledge Networking*. Boston: Butterworth–Heinemann.

Schein, Edgar H. 1991. "What is Culture?" In Frost, Moore et al., *Reframing Organizational Culture*. Newbury Park, Calif.: Sage.

Schön, Donald A. 1983. *The Reflective Practitioner: How Professionals Think in Action*. New York: Basic Books.

Selznick, Philip. 1957. *Leadership in Administration: A Sociological Interpretation*. New York: Harper & Row.

Senge, Peter M. 1990. *The Fifth Discipline: The Art and Practice of the Learning Organization*. New York: Doubleday/Century Business.

Shannon, Claude E., and Warren Weaver. 1959. *The Mathematical Theory of Communication*. Urbana: University of Illinois Press.

Stewart, Thomas A. 1994. "Your Company's Most Valuable Asset: Intellectual Capital." *Fortune* 130 (October 3):68–74.

Sveiby, Karl Erik, and Anders Risling. 1986. *Kunskapsföretaget (The Know-How Company)*. Malmö: Liber.

Sveiby, Karl Erik, and Tom Lloyd. 1987. *Managing Knowhow: Add Value . . . by Valuing Creativity.* London: Bloomsbury.

Sveiby, Karl Erik et al. 1988. *Den Nya Årsredovisningen (The New Annual Report).* Stockholm: Affärsvärlden.

Sveiby, Karl Erik et al. 1989. *Den Osynliga Balansräkningen (The Invisible Balance Sheet).* Stockholm: Affärsvärlden/Ledarskap.

Sveiby, Karl Erik. 1990. *Kunskapsledning (Knowledge Management).* Stockholm: Affärsvärlden/Ledarskap.

Sveiby, Karl Erik. 1994. "Towards a Knowledge Perspective on Organization." Ph.D. diss., University of Stockholm.

Toffler, Alvin. 1980. *The Third Wave.* New York: Morrow.

Weber, Max. 1986. *Kapitalismens uppkomst (The Protestant Ethic and the Spirit of Capitalism).* Stockholm: Ratio.

Weick, Karl E. 1977. "Enactment Processes in Organizations." In *New Directions in Organizational Behavior,* edited by Barry M. Staw and Gerald R. Salancik. Chicago: St. Clair Press.

Weick, Karl E. 1983. "Managerial Thought in the Context of Action." In *The Executive Mind,* edited by Suresh Srivastva. San Francisco: Jossey–Bass.

Wheatley, Margaret J. 1992. *Leadership and the New Science: Learning about Organization from an Orderly Universe.* San Francisco: Berrett–Koehler.

Wiener, Norbert. 1948. *Cybernetics; or, Control and Communication in the Animal and the Machine.* Cambridge, Mass.: Technology Press.

Wittgenstein, Ludwig. 1962. *Tractatus Logico-Philosophicus.* (English version). Stockholm: Orion.

Wittgenstein, Ludwig. 1995. *Philosophical Investigations.* (orig. 1953). London, England: Blackwell.

Womack, James P., Daniel T. Jones, and Daniel Roos. 1990. *The Machine That Changed the World: Based on the Massachusetts Institute of Technology 5 Million Dollar 5 Year Study on the Future of the Automobile.* New York: Rawson Associates.

Zuboff, Shoshana. 1988. *In the Age of the Smart Machine: The Future of Work and Power.* New York: Basic Books.

This section lists all of the writings used by the author in preparing this book; however, readers researching the topic of Knowledge Organizations should be aware that some of the references listed are not widely available in the United States. Many of the books published in Sweden are available at the University of Stockholm library or directly from the publishers.

Index

About the Author

Dr. Karl Erik Sveiby became acutely aware of knowledge management when he and his partners bought out the business journal *Affärsvärlden* in 1979. With everything outsourced except the editorial work, it was a business with only intangible assets. It resembled nothing he had experienced during his years as a manager at Unilever, nor had the university curriculum prepared him for it.

His quest to understand his new business led him to develop a new way of viewing the firm—as a knowledge organization. Subsequent years saw Dr. Sveiby and his partners develop *Affärsvärlden* into Ekonomi + Teknik Frlag, one of the largest trade publishers in Scandinavia, offering a broad spectrum of journals and information services.

Dr. Sveiby's first book, published in 1986 and co-authored with Anders Risling, was titled *Kunskapsföretaget (The Know-How Company)*. The book became a bestseller in Scandinavia and inspired numerous researchers and practitioners to develop the principles further. A unique dialogue between theory and practice emerged with a Swedish community of practice in the field of managing and measuring intangible assets.

One of the project groups that Dr. Sveiby convened developed a method for measuring intangible assets based on his concepts. The group's proposals, outlined in *Den Nya Arsredovisningen (The New Annual Report*, Sveiby et al. 1988) and *Den Osynliga Balansräkningen (The Invisible Balance Sheet*, Sveiby et al. 1989), were widely used by Swedish companies, and in 1994 the Swedish Council of Service Industries recommended that its members use them in their annual reports. Public companies in Sweden today are world pioneers in the public reporting of intangible assets and Sweden has become the greatest proponent of the knowledge management and intellectual capital movements.

Dr. Sveiby's other books include the following: *Kunskapsledning (Knowledge Management)*, awarded Best Management Book in Sweden (1990); *Chef i kreativ milj (Manager in Creative Environments*, 1991); *Kunskapsfldet (The Flow of Knowledge*, 1994) awarded Honorable Mention, 1995); *Kunskap r Makt (Knowledge Is Power*, 1994); *The Knowledge Organization: An Introduction* (1994); *Kreativitet och Makt (Creativity and Power*, 1994); and *Rikspolisstyrelsen* (1994).

In 1993 Dr. Sveiby and his partners sold their company. In 1994, Dr. Sveiby finished his Ph.D. at Stockholm University with a thesis entitled "Toward a Knowledge Perspective on Organization." Today Dr. Sveiby is advisor to knowledge organizations all over the world. He and his family currently live in Brisbane, Australia.

Berrett-Koehler Publishers

BERRETT-KOEHLER is an independent publisher of books, periodicals, and other publications at the leading edge of new thinking and innovative practice on work, business, management, leadership, stewardship, career development, human resources, entrepreneurship, and global sustainability.

Since the company's founding in 1992, we have been committed to supporting the movement toward a more enlightened world of work by publishing books, periodicals, and other publications that help us to integrate our values with our work and work lives, and to create more humane and effective organizations.

We have chosen to focus on the areas of work, business, and organizations, because these are central elements in many people's lives today. Furthermore, the work world is going through tumultuous changes, from the decline of job security to the rise of new structures for organizing people and work. We believe that change is needed at all levels—individual, organizational, community, and global—and our publications address each of these levels.

We seek to create new lenses for understanding organizations, to legitimize topics that people care deeply about but that current business orthodoxy censors or considers secondary to bottom-line concerns, and to uncover new meaning, means, and ends for our work and work lives.

See next page for other books from Berrett-Koehler Publishers

Other leading-edge business books
from Berrett-Koehler Publishers

The Intelligent Organization
Engaging the Talent and Initiative of
Everyone in the Workplace
Gifford and Elizabeth Pinchot

THIS BOOK shows how to replace bureaucracy with more humane and effective systems for organizing and coordinating work. The Pinchots show how, by engaging the intelligence, business judgment, and wide-system responsibility of all its members, an organization can respond more effectively to customers, partners, and competitors.

Paperback, 420 pages, 10/96 • ISBN 1-881052-98-2 CIP
Item no. 52982-177 $19.95

Hardcover, 3/94 • ISBN 1-881052-34-6 CIP • **Item no. 52346-177 $24.95**

The New Management
Democracy and Enterprise
Are Transforming Organizations
William E. Halal

THE NEW MANAGEMENT integrates emerging practices into a coherent, clarifying whole. Drawing on hundreds of examples from progressive companies, an international survey of 426 managers, and economic trends, William Halal shows how enterprise and democracy are moving inside of business and government to transform institutions for the Information Age.

Hardcover, 300 pages, 5/96 • ISBN 1-881052-53-2 CIP
Item no. 52532-177 $29.95

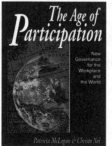

The Age of Participation
New Governance for the Workplace
and the World
by Patricia McLagan and Christo Nel

BLENDING THEORY and practice, providing numerous examples, and drawing on more than forty years of experience in over 200 organizations, McLagan and Nel describe what executives, managers, workers, labor unions, customers, and suppliers can do as part of a participative enterprise.

Hardcover, 300 pages, 9/95 • ISBN 1-881052-56-7 CIP
Item no. 52567-177 $27.95

Available at your favorite bookstore, or call (800) 929-2929

The Fourth Wave
Business in the 21st Century

Herman Bryant Maynard, Jr. and Susan E. Mehrtens

APPLYING THE CONCEPT of historical waves propounded by Alvin Toffler in *The Third Wave,* Herman Maynard and Susan Mehrtens look foresee a "fourth wave," an era of integration and responsibility. They examine how business has changed in the second and third waves and must continue to change in the fourth—how an institution is organized, defines wealth, relates to surrounding communities, responds to environmental needs, and takes part in the political process.

Paperback, 236 pages, 7/96 • ISBN 1-57675-002-7
Item no. 50027-177 $18.95

Hardcover, 6/93 • ISBN 1-881052-15-X • **Item no. 5215X-177 $28.95**

Leadership and the New Science
Learning about Organization from an Orderly Universe

Margaret J. Wheatley

"The Best Management Book of the Year!"
—*Industry Week* magazine survey by Tom Brown

OUR UNDERSTANDING of the universe is being radically altered by revolutionary discoveries in quantum physics, chaos theory, and evolutionary biology that are overturning the prevailing models of science. Wheatley shows how the "New Science" provides powerful insights for changing how we design, lead, and view organizations.

Paperback, 172 pages, 3/94 • ISBN 1-881052-44-3 CIP
Item no. 52443-177 $15.95

Hardcover, 9/92 • ISBN 1-881052-01-X CIP • **Item no. 5201X-177 $24.95**

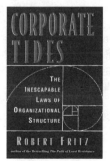

Corporate Tides
The Inescapable Laws of Organizational Structure

Robert Fritz

CORPORATE LEADERS waste billions of dollars each year on attempts to change organizations through programs that were doomed before they started. In *Corporate Tides,* Robert Fritz addresses the fundamental causes of organizational success or failure. Fritz shows that once structural forces are understood and structural principles applied within the organization, managers can achieve real, lasting success for the company.

Hardcover, 200 pages, June 1996 • ISBN 1-881052-88-5
Item no. 52885-177 $27.95

Available at your favorite bookstore, or call (800) 929-2929

Software to help you measure and manage your intangible assets

The Intangible Assets Monitor
How to Measure and Manage Knowledge-Based Assets

Karl Erik Sveiby (produced by LearnerFirst)

MANY MANAGEMENT EXPERTS and top executives believe that knowledge management is an essential part of business strategy. The Intangible Assets Monitor is the first practical tool for measuring and managing knowledge.

Based on the Intangible Assets Monitor presented in Karl Erik Sveiby's book, *The New Organizational Wealth,* and produced by LearnerFirst in conjunction with Dr. Sveiby, the Monitor strips away the shroud of confusion surrounding the area of knowledge management. It provides individualized guidance for creating and evolving organization-specific measures.

Sveiby's Monitor is based on an approach which has been proven effective in dozens of organizations. The Monitor is operationalized in a unique software application which supports learning and doing.

Available Summer 1997
For information on pricing and configuration, please visit
the LearnerFirst web site at www.learnerfirst.com

Tango business simulation offers hands-on experience with managing and measuring intangible assets

TANGO™ is a business simulation that brings the concepts outlined in Karl Erik Sveiby's book, *The New Organizational Wealth,* into practical action. Participants learn to apply a knowledge-focused strategy to manage and measure knowledge-based assets.

Working in four-member management teams, participants are run a fictional company for seven annual cycles, pursuing its business strategy in order to maximize the market value of their tangible and intangible assets. Each team competes with the other teams for the same customers and key personnel.

Tango is a two-day workshop that was developed by Klas Mellander, Celemi Sweden, and Karl Erik Sveiby.

For further information, please contact:
Celemi Inc.   1 Grist Mill Road   Simsbury, CT 06070
Tel: (860) 651-7595   Toll free: (800)796-1112   Fax: (860)651-4179
celemius@celemi.se

CELEMI
THE POWER OF LEARNING

If you like the ideas in *The New Organizational Wealth* and are interested in joining a discussion group to explore them with others, please fill out the form below and mail or fax it to:

Berrett-Koehler Publishers
450 Sansome Street, Suite 1200
San Francisco, CA 94111
Tel: (415) 288-0260
Fax: (415) 362-2512
bkpub@aol.com

Name _____

Title _____

Company _____

Address

_____

Tel _____

Fax _____

Email _____

Where did you buy this book?_____